THE STANDARD FOR
EARNED VALUE MANAGEMENT

Library of Congress Cataloging-in-Publication Data

Names: Project Management Institute, issuing body.
Title: The standard for earned value management / Project Management Institute. Description: Newtown Square : Project Management Institute, Inc., 2019. | Includes bibliographical references and index. | Summary: "Earned value management (EVM) is a management methodology for integrating scope, schedule, and resources; objectively measuring project performance and progress; and forecasting project outcome. It is considered by many to be one of the most effective performance measurement and feedback tools for managing projects. The Standard for Earned Value Management builds on the concepts for EVM described in the Practice Standard for Earned Value Management and includes enhanced project delivery information, by integrating concepts and practices from the PMBOK® Guide - Sixth Edition and The Agile Practice Guide. A central theme in this standard is the recognition that the definition for value in EVM has expanded. While the term retains its traditional definition in terms of project cost, it embraces current practice by including the concept of earned schedule. This standard also integrates hybrid methodologies that blend together historical EVM concepts with the needs of the agile practitioner, all with an eye towards aiding the project team in enhancing overall project delivery. This standard is a useful tool for experienced project management practitioners who are seeking to expand and update their knowledge of the field as well as less experienced practitioners who want to learn other approaches for managing project performance. It provides insight and detailed explanations of the basic elements and processes of EVM, and demonstrates how to scale EVM to fit varying project sizes and situations. This standard includes graphical examples and detailed explanations that will enable the reader to establish and implement EVM on projects in almost any environment and of almost every size. When used together with good project management principles, EVM methodology will provide a greater return on any project and results that will directly benefit your organization"-- Provided by publisher.
Identifiers: LCCN 2019044299 (print) | LCCN 2019044300 (ebook) | ISBN
    9781628256383 (paperback) | ISBN 9781628256390 (epub) | ISBN
    9781628256406 (kindle edition) | ISBN 9781628256413 (pdf)
Subjects: LCSH: Project management--Standards. | Project management--Methodology.
Classification: LCC HD69.P75 S734 2019 (print) | LCC HD69.P75 (ebook) | DDC
    658.4/04--dc23
LC record available at https://lccn.loc.gov/2019044299
LC ebook record available at https://lccn.loc.gov/2019044300

ISBN: 978-1-62825-638-3

Published by:
    Project Management Institute, Inc.
    14 Campus Boulevard
    Newtown Square, Pennsylvania 19073-3299 USA
    Phone: +610-356-4600
    Fax: +610-356-4647
    Email: customercare@pmi.org
    Internet: www.PMI.org

To place a Trade Order or for pricing information, please contact Independent Publishers Group:
    Independent Publishers Group
    Order Department
    814 North Franklin Street
    Chicago, IL 60610 USA
    Phone: +1 800-888-4741
    Fax: +1 312-337-5985
    Email: orders@ipgbook.com (For orders only)

For all other inquiries, please contact the PMI Book Service Center.
    PMI Book Service Center
    P.O. Box 932683, Atlanta, GA 31193-2683 USA
    Phone: 1-866-276-4764 (within the U.S. or Canada) or +1-770-280-4129 (globally)
    Fax: +1-770-280-4113
    Email: info@bookorders.pmi.org

10 9 8 7 6 5 4 3 2 1

NOTICE

The Project Management Institute, Inc. (PMI) standards and guideline publications, of which the document contained herein is one, are developed through a voluntary consensus standards development process. This process brings together volunteers and/or seeks out the views of persons who have an interest in the topic covered by this publication. While PMI administers the process and establishes rules to promote fairness in the development of consensus, it does not write the document and it does not independently test, evaluate, or verify the accuracy or completeness of any information or the soundness of any judgments contained in its standards and guideline publications.

PMI disclaims liability for any personal injury, property or other damages of any nature whatsoever, whether special, indirect, consequential or compensatory, directly or indirectly resulting from the publication, use of application, or reliance on this document. PMI disclaims and makes no guaranty or warranty, expressed or implied, as to the accuracy or completeness of any information published herein, and disclaims and makes no warranty that the information in this document will fulfill any of your particular purposes or needs. PMI does not undertake to guarantee the performance of any individual manufacturer or seller's products or services by virtue of this standard or guide.

In publishing and making this document available, PMI is not undertaking to render professional or other services for or on behalf of any person or entity, nor is PMI undertaking to perform any duty owed by any person or entity to someone else. Anyone using this document should rely on his or her own independent judgment or, as appropriate, seek the advice of a competent professional in determining the exercise of reasonable care in any given circumstances. Information and other standards on the topic covered by this publication may be available from other sources, which the user may wish to consult for additional views or information not covered by this publication.

PMI has no power, nor does it undertake to police or enforce compliance with the contents of this document. PMI does not certify, test, or inspect products, designs, or installations for safety or health purposes. Any certification or other statement of compliance with any health or safety-related information in this document shall not be attributable to PMI and is solely the responsibility of the certifier or maker of the statement.

TABLE OF CONTENTS

LIST OF FIGURES AND TABLES

1

INTRODUCTION

1.1 PURPOSE OF *THE STANDARD FOR EARNED VALUE MANAGEMENT*

This standard provides a perspective of earned value management (EVM) that is consistent with current practice. This update to the former practice guide broadens the perspectives regarding the choices and decisions about the optimal approach for the planning and delivery of projects. This in turn supports the ability of the project team and their stakeholders to tailor their planning, management, and delivery implementation framework accordingly. This standard provides guidance on the use of EVM in agile, hybrid, and predictive contexts.

The *PMI Lexicon of Project Management Terms* [1][1] defines EVM as a methodology that combines scope, schedule, and resource measurements to assess project performance and progress. An earned value management system (EVMS) is a set of principles, methods, processes, practices, and tools for managing project performance. When EVM is used in concert with the Process Groups, Knowledge Areas, and processes defined in *A Guide to the Project Management Body of Knowledge (PMBOK® Guide)* [2], the project manager, the broader project team, and relevant stakeholders will be able to understand project progress and gain insight into future performance based on the analysis and interpretation of project performance information. The use of EVM improves the overall project delivery process through increased insight into efficiencies, opportunities, risk management, and better project outcomes.

This standard was developed with the project manager, project team, and stakeholders as the primary beneficiaries. The purpose of this standard is to provide information and guidance for the project team to help identify and implement practices and processes that enhance and improve project delivery.

---

[1] The numbers in brackets refer to the list of references at the end of this standard.

This standard has been guided by the following principles:

◆ Scope, schedule, and cost are three interrelated aspects of a single, integrated performance measurement baseline (PMB). The PMB is defined in the *Lexicon* as the integrated scope, cost, and schedule baselines used to manage, measure, and control project execution.

◆ Traditionally, earned value (work performed) is defined in monetary terms, but it may be expressed in other units that are more relevant for a specific project (units of time, story points, etc.). The units selected would depend on the nature of the project and the priorities of the sponsoring entity.

◆ The use of EVM is relevant to all service delivery and product development projects, irrespective of the use of predictive or iterative adaptive approaches. Vocabulary and graphical conventions vary, but the core principles and meanings are consistent and apply independently of development life-cycle choices.

◆ Plan performance assessment and the causal analysis of variances to plan are key elements of the EVM implementation and inform the development of recovery plans, as appropriate.

◆ Baseline changes are formally documented and approved.

◆ Project forecasting is informed by the analysis of past performance as well as monitoring of the project environment.

◆ Performance information is used to manage and report performance on the project.

1.2 STRUCTURE OF THIS STANDARD

This standard addresses the Initiating, Planning, Executing, Monitoring and Controlling, and Closing Process Groups in an EVM context. The structure of this standard is intended to be compatible with the *PMBOK® Guide* concepts and principles when a more structured EVM approach is desired by the project team. Additional interpretation of the *PMBOK® Guide* is provided, when needed, to illustrate the intent of this standard. Subsequent sections are:

◆ **Section 2.** Initiating

◆ **Section 3.** Planning

◆ **Section 4.** Executing, Monitoring, and Controlling

◆ **Section 5.** Closing

The appendixes included in this standard are:

◆ **Appendix X1.** Development of *The Standard for Earned Value Management*

◆ **Appendix X2.** Contributors and Reviewers of *The Standard for Earned Value Management*

◆ **Appendix X3**. Application of Earned Value Management (EVM) at the Portfolio and Program Levels

◆ **Appendix X4**. Performance Management Example

1.3 WHAT IS EARNED VALUE MANAGEMENT (EVM)?

1.3.1 EVM OVERVIEW

For purposes of extending the thought leadership and use of EVM across the profession, it is useful to extend the PMB concept to a sophisticated approach for project integration management. This in turn is based on a time-phased, integrated performance management baseline that incorporates project scope, schedule, and resource measurements to assess project performance and progress. EVM helps to identify the causes of deviations from the baseline that may need recovery planning. Moreover, EVM informs the process for estimating project outcomes based on both past performance and current project conditions.

It is possible to represent status and projections in each of the cost, schedule, and scope aspects of the project. Historical practice has translated all expressions of status versus baseline to a financial value, including schedule impacts. Representation in the time dimension of the baseline is a key element of earned schedule (ES). Likewise, reflecting project progress in terms of scope is often done using burn charts and backlog in agile or hybrid environments.

The application of earned value analysis in the early phases of a project increases the usefulness of the scope, schedule, and cost baselines by adding performance measurement. Once established, this integrated baseline underpins the understanding of project performance during the complete project life cycle. A comparison of actual performance and realization of value against the integrated baseline provides:

◆ Feedback on the project's current status compared to baseline, and

◆ Insight into future performance.

EVM permits a project to be measured by progress achieved and enables the estimation of probable outcomes to make timely and useful decisions using objective data. At any time during any project phase, earned value analysis informs answers to the following questions:

◆ What has been achieved with the resources that have been applied?

◆ What is the anticipated endpoint position?

1.3.2 A SYSTEMS VIEW OF EVM

Practitioners are often involved with change initiatives and project-based work in a complex environment with overlapping and conflicting interests. For practitioners to comprehend such situations and be in a position to anticipate behaviors and performance trends, it is necessary to analyze portfolios, programs, and projects as systems. In addition to examining and understanding the parts of the system individually, practitioners also analyze and understand the whole system in question. It is important to be aware of the causes and effects of the interactions of the system's parts or components. In other words, practitioners need to understand interdependencies—the interactions between components of the system as well as the interrelationships between components of the system and its organizational environment. Project managers should have (a) a good understanding of the business and/or use case, (b) the connection of project performance with the organizational strategy and environment, and (c) the ability to communicate the plan to the team.

EVM is one of the most effective performance measurement and feedback tools for the project management discipline. The earned value (EV) concept relates budget, actual cost, and actual work progress in one integrated system that provides a reliable projection of future project performance. This fundamental principle may be extended to portfolios and programs. Feedback is critical to the successful management of any portfolio, program, or project. Timely and targeted feedback enables practitioners to identify issues early and inform the project delivery process.

Without reliable inputs of planned value (PV), actual cost (AC), and earned value (EV, EVM is unlikely to succeed. To gather these inputs, practitioners should carefully scope, budget, and schedule, and then monitor a project throughout the entire project life cycle as described in detail in both the *PMBOK® Guide* and the *Agile Practice Guide* [3]. In brief, projects using EVM should:

- First identify the work content and requirements using a work breakdown structure (WBS).

- Plan the project to form a PMB. Carefully monitor the progress of actual work and the costs associated with this progress so that EV and AC data can be obtained.

- Manage projects through integrated change control, which directly impacts the project scope, budget, schedule, and the associated PMB. When changes are managed properly, the PMB remains a constant and traceable source of information with high integrity to manage and assess project performance.

EVM emphasizes the importance of other key considerations necessary for successful project management. These include organizational structure, cost collection methodologies, and the process for managing project changes. EVM provides organizations with a thoughtful methodology to integrate the management of project scope, schedule, and resources. This standard uses the term *project scope* to mean the work performed to deliver a product, service, or result with the specified features and functions. EVM can be used to answer questions that are critical to the success of every project, such as:

◆ Are we delivering more or less work than planned?

◆ When will the project finish?

◆ When is the project likely to be completed?

◆ Are we currently over or under budget?

◆ What is the remaining work likely to cost?

◆ What is the entire project likely to cost?

◆ How much will the project be over or under budget at the end of the project?

◆ How much effort is required to complete the project?

◆ What is driving the significant cost and/or schedule variances?

A fundamental concept of EVM is that patterns and trends of accomplished performance, when compared against a sound baseline, produce reliable forecasts of a project's future performance.

1.3.3 EVM AND PROJECT MANAGEMENT

The practice of EVM is consistent with good project management as outlined in the *PMBOK® Guide* and the *Agile Practice Guide*. Table 1-1 maps the processes from the *PMBOK® Guide* by Project Management Process Groups and Knowledge Areas (the section numbers listed are from the *PMBOK® Guide*). EVM is applicable to all of the Project Management Process Groups and Knowledge Areas described in the *PMBOK® Guide* and can be used to amplify the project management practice.

As a performance management methodology, EVM adds some critical practices to the project management processes. These practices occur within the Process Groups of Initiating, Planning, Executing, and Monitoring and Controlling and are related to the goal of measuring, analyzing, forecasting, and reporting project cost and schedule.

Measuring, forecasting, and continually improving project performance are the foundational requirements that underpin EVM. The additional effort invested for a proper and right-sized EVMS can deliver a positive return on that investment.

Table 1-1. Project Management Process Groups and Knowledge Areas (Source: *PMBOK® Guide*)

Knowledge Areas	Project Management Process Groups				
	Initiating Process Group	Planning Process Group	Executing Process Group	Monitoring and Controlling Process Group	Closing Process Group
4. Project Integration Management	4.1 Develop Project Charter	4.2 Develop Project Management Plan	4.3 Direct and Manage Project Work 4.4 Manage Project Knowledge	4.5 Monitor and Control Project Work 4.6 Perform Integrated Change Control	4.7 Close Project or Phase
5. Project Scope Management		5.1 Plan Scope Management 5.2 Collect Requirements 5.3 Define Scope 5.4 Create WBS		5.5 Validate Scope 5.6 Control Scope	
6. Project Schedule Management		6.1 Plan Schedule Management 6.2 Define Activities 6.3 Sequence Activities 6.4 Estimate Activity Durations 6.5 Develop Schedule		6.6 Control Schedule	
7. Project Cost Management		7.1 Plan Cost Management 7.2 Estimate Costs 7.3 Determine Budget		7.4 Control Costs	
8. Project Quality Management		8.1 Plan Quality Management	8.2 Manage Quality	8.3 Control Quality	
9. Project Resource Management		9.1 Plan Resource Management 9.2 Estimate Activity Resources	9.3 Acquire Resources 9.4 Develop Team 9.5 Manage Team	9.6 Control Resources	
10. Project Communications Management		10.1 Plan Communications Management	10.2 Manage Communications	10.3 Monitor Communications	
11. Project Risk Management		11.1 Plan Risk Management 11.2 Identify Risks 11.3 Perform Qualitative Risk Analysis 11.4 Perform Quantitative Risk Analysis 11.5 Plan Risk Responses	11.6 Implement Risk Responses	11.7 Monitor Risks	
12. Project Procurement Management		12.1 Plan Procurement Management	12.2 Conduct Procurements	12.3 Control Procurements	
13. Project Stakeholder Management	13.1 Identify Stakeholders	13.2 Plan Stakeholder Engagement	13.3 Manage Stakeholder Engagement	13.4 Monitor Stakeholder Engagement	

EVM requires accurate and reliable information. EVM performance measures used in conjunction with the project's WBS provide the objective data and information needed to produce sound information for good project management decision making. Variance analysis metrics, in absolute value or percentages, and cost/schedule efficiency indices are used most often. With an EVMS, the project team may be held accountable for reporting, diagnosing, and explaining the causes of past performance of the project using EVM analysis data and information. The project team may also be responsible for making forecasts of the possible outcomes for the project or project phase, which entails explaining the cost, schedule, and at-completion variances, as well as devising effective interventions aimed at improving performance.

A properly designed and implemented EVMS that meets the particular requirements of an organization may yield considerable benefits in measuring productivity and improved forecasting in all project-based work. Decades of research have proven that the application of EVM principles and practices are positive predictors of project success. For projects in which the application of EVM processes are not part of a contract, practitioners may want to be innovative toward optimizing the implementation with an eye toward schedule, costs, and benefits. In such projects, practitioners may plan an EVM process that complies with the foundational requirements while capturing and processing the minimum essential data for the particular project. Practitioners may find it beneficial to communicate and demonstrate to the project sponsor, governance, and senior management about the value of incorporating EVM as a primary performance management methodology within the organization.

1.3.4 PRINCIPAL EVM TERMINOLOGY AND METRICS

EVM methodology is described in the *PMBOK® Guide* and is further elaborated in this standard. Throughout this standard, terminology that is unique to EVM is used frequently. All of the EVM terms used in this standard are included in the glossary. Definitions of the three most important terms used in EVM are:

- ◆ **Earned value (EV).** The measure of the work performed, expressed in terms of the budget authorized for that work. EV can be reported for cumulative to date or for a specific reporting period.

- ◆ **Planned value (PV).** The authorized budget assigned to scheduled work. The total budgeted cost of the planned work. At any point in time, PV defines the work that should have been accomplished. PV can be reported for cumulative work to date or for a specific reporting period.

- ◆ **Actual cost (AC).** The cost incurred while performing the activity. Cost for the work performed on an activity during a specific time period. This can be reported for cumulative to date or for a specific reporting period (as cash flow or an S-curve).

Table 1-2 incorporates the principal EVM terminology, interrelationships, and calculations.

Table 1-2. Earned Value Calculations Summary Table (Source: *PMBOK® Guide* – Sixth Edition)

Earned Value Analysis					
Abbreviation	Name	Lexicon Definition	How Used	Equation	Interpretation of Result
PV	Planned Value	The authorized budget assigned to scheduled work.	The value of the work planned to be completed to a point in time, usually the data date, or project completion.		
EV	Earned Value	The measure of work performed expressed in terms of the budget authorized for that work.	The planned value of all the work completed (earned) to a point in time, usually the data date, without reference to actual costs.	EV = sum of the planned value of completed work	
AC	Actual Cost	The realized cost incurred for the work performed on an activity during a specific time period.	The actual cost of all the work completed to a point in time, usually the data date.		
BAC	Budget at Completion	The sum of all budgets established for the work to be performed.	The value of total planned work, the project cost baseline.		
CV	Cost Variance	The amount of budget deficit or surplus at a given point in time, expressed as the difference between the earned value and the actual cost.	The difference between the value of work completed to a point in time, usually the data date, and the actual costs to the same point in time.	CV = EV – AC	Positive = Under planned cost Neutral = On planned cost Negative = Over planned cost
SV	Schedule Variance	The amount by which the project is ahead or behind the planned delivery date, at a given point in time, expressed as the difference between the earned value and the planned value.	The difference between the work completed to a point in time, usually the data date, and the work planned to be completed to the same point in time.	SV = EV – PV	Positive = Ahead of schedule Neutral = On schedule Negative = Behind schedule
VAC	Variance at Completion	A projection of the amount of budget deficit or surplus, expressed as the difference between the budget at completion and the estimate at completion.	The estimated difference in cost at the completion of the project.	VAC = BAC – EAC	Positive = Under planned cost Neutral = On planned cost Negative = Over planned cost
CPI	Cost Performance Index	A measure of the cost efficiency of budgeted resources expressed as the ratio of earned value to actual cost.	A CPI of 1.0 means the project is exactly on budget, that the work actually done so far is exactly the same as the cost so far. Other values show the percentage of how much costs are over or under the budgeted amount for work accomplished.	CPI = EV/AC	Greater than 1.0 = Under planned cost Exactly 1.0 = On planned cost Less than 1.0 = Over planned cost
SPI	Schedule Performance Index	A measure of schedule efficiency expressed as the ratio of earned value to planned value.	An SPI of 1.0 means that the project is exactly on schedule, that the work actually done so far is exactly the same as the work planned to be done so far. Other values show the percentage of how much costs are over or under the budgeted amount for work planned.	SPI = EV/PV	Greater than 1.0 = Ahead of schedule Exactly 1.0 = On schedule Less than 1.0 = Behind schedule
EAC	Estimate at Completion	The expected total cost of completing all work expressed as the sum of the actual cost to date and the estimate to complete.	If the CPI is expected to be the same for the remainder of the project, EAC can be calculated using: If future work will be accomplished at the planned rate, use: If the initial plan is no longer valid, use: If both the CPI and SPI influence the remaining work, use:	EAC = BAC/CPI EAC = AC + BAC – EV EAC = AC + Bottom-up ETC EAC = AC + [(BAC – EV)/ (CPI x SPI)]	
ETC	Estimate to Complete	The expected cost to finish all the remaining project work.	Assuming work is proceeding on plan, the cost of completing the remaining authorized work can be calculated using: Reestimate the remaining work from the bottom up.	ETC = EAC – AC ETC = Reestimate	
TCPI	To Complete Performance Index	A measure of the cost performance that must be achieved with the remaining resources in order to meet a specified management goal, expressed as the ratio of the cost to finish the outstanding work to the budget available.	The efficiency that must be maintained in order to complete on plan. The efficiency that must be maintained in order to complete the current EAC.	TCPI = (BAC–EV)/(BAC–AC) TCPI = (BAC – EV)/(EAC–AC)	Greater than 1.0 = Harder to complete Exactly 1.0 = Same to complete Less than 1.0 = Easier to complete Greater than 1.0 = Harder to complete Exactly 1.0 = Same to complete Less than 1.0 = Easier to complete

Within the practice of project management, developments include the expansion of EVM to include the concept of earned schedule (ES). ES is an extension to the theory and practice of EVM. ES adds to the schedule management. ES concepts and practices are described in Sections 3 and 4 of this standard.

1.4 BASIC EVM CONCEPTS

Effective planning requires a firm understanding of assumptions, requirements, constraints, scope, and deliverables. In an agile or in a hybrid environment, these may include burn charts and velocity calculations. Planning also includes the development of the various project management plans and is where the initial identification as to how and when EVM will be done for a specific project takes place. During the planning process, the means for assessing physical work progress and assigning EV has to be documented.

During the planning process, the emphasis is placed on gaining agreement among the principal stakeholders regarding the project objectives. Using a WBS, at this point, the scope of the project needs to be elaborated into executable and manageable parts known as work packages (WP). Aligning the WPs defined in the WBS into project cost and scheduling subsystems is a project management practice. The WPs may be organized in control accounts (CAs) based on the project organizational breakdown structure (OBS) and responsibility assignment matrix (RAM). A CA is a management control point where scope, budget, and schedule are integrated and compared to the EV for performance measurement.

Project work needs to be scheduled up to the completion of the project, including the identification of critical milestones. The project schedule shows the timing of key accomplishments and interfaces. It also provides evidence that the project management plan supports the stakeholder agreement regarding project objectives. Scheduling cannot be executed without knowledge of resource availability and constraints. This is an iterative process until a balance is struck that meets project scheduling objectives within the identified resource limitations.

Once the work is logically scheduled and resources identified, the work scope, schedule, and cost are integrated and recorded in a time-phased budget known as the PMB. This is the time-phased budget plan that is used to measure project performance. In addition to routine project management planning, EVM methods are selected and applied for each CA or WP based on scope, schedule, and cost considerations.

During project execution, EVM requires the recording of resource utilization (labor, materials, etc.) and risk response cost for the work performed within each of the work elements in the project management plan. In other words, actual costs need to be captured in a way (both per the WBS and the calendar) that permits comparison with the PMB. Actual costs are collected at the CA level or below. The whole process is explained in detail in Sections 3 and 4 of this standard.

In the project control process, EVM requires physical work progress assessment as well as the assessment of EV (using a combination of domain- and product-specific measures, quality control procedures, and earned value analysis). With these EV data—the planned value (PV) data (from the PMB) and the actual cost (AC) data (from the project cost tracking system)—the project team performs earned value analysis at the CA level (or any other levels of the project WBS). In addition, this analysis can be used to develop recovery action plans (preventive and corrective) for any discovered issues or risks and update the forecast of expected project outcomes at completion. Moreover, the information elicited from the earned value analysis also adds to the lessons learned documents of the project.

Approved project changes, either driven by stakeholders external to the project team (e.g., from the project's change control board [CCB] or by the project team itself), are implemented into the project baseline in a timely and accurate fashion using the change control system established for the project. The same care taken to initially establish the PMB needs to be continued to maintain a valid PMB throughout the life of the project. An upheld valid PMB also involves the use of maintained configuration management knowledge repositories of the project.

1.5 RELATIONSHIP WITH PORTFOLIOS AND PROGRAMS

1.5.1 THE DOMAINS OF PORTFOLIO AND PROGRAM MANAGEMENT

A *portfolio* is a collection of projects, programs, subsidiary portfolios, and operations managed as a group to achieve strategic objectives. The purpose of portfolio execution is to accomplish strategic objectives and add value to the organization. At the portfolio level, the addition of value needs to be recognized and measured. Reliable metrics are required for this. Portfolio practitioners need to clearly define units of measurement, a baseline to measure portfolio performance from, and apply proven methods toward making the performance measurements. Metrics related to the addition of value for the whole portfolio may attach to tangible and intangible business outcomes—the sum of all portfolio acquired benefits minus all portfolio resource expenditures. One of the usual metrics is the performance achieved by the outputs and the resulting benefits generated by the components in the portfolio.

Portfolios provide organizations with the means to execute strategies. Organizational strategies are pursued using programs and projects sponsored within the portfolio. Programs and projects pursue strategies of change and produce the benefits and outcomes required for achieving an organization's strategy; they also add value to the organization. Program and project management enable organizations to successfully release and deliver the selected business value opportunities. Performance management lies across the entire management function and critically enhances the ability to realize the envisioned business value. At all levels, EV is a key performance measurement process.

As mentioned previously in this section, practitioners may use the application of EVM as a reliable, proven performance metric for portfolio and program components' performance. It is also beneficial when portfolio practitioners use EVM for measuring the performance of their whole portfolio system. Such analysis requires the application of EV concepts at the portfolio level. Managing a portfolio is about maximizing the delivery of value (instead of the delivery of scope at the project level) through the execution of portfolio components aligned to organizational strategy and strategic objectives.

In addition to aggregating portfolio components' EV metrics for the whole portfolio, portfolio management teams may decide to create overall value realization metrics for the portfolio system. To create these, they need to:

◆ Determine and get approval from portfolio governance as to what is most important to measure.

◆ Create a realistic measurement method.

◆ Set a time-phased baseline for the portfolio parameters to be measured.

◆ Take measurements from this baseline at regular time intervals to identify variances.

◆ Create performance indicators that depict the recorded metrics. At the portfolio level, different indicators than the ones used for project management need to be created.

A *program* is defined as a group of related projects, subsidiary programs, and program activities managed in a coordinated manner to obtain benefits not available from managing them individually. Programs are conducted primarily to deliver benefits to sponsoring organizations. As executable program components begin to deliver, it becomes possible to create performance metrics for the benefits of those deliverables. Performance metrics, such as the establishment of an EVMS, enhance effective decision making at both the governance and management levels in order to reprioritize, reschedule, or reevaluate resources. Performance metrics for each of the program's component projects should be provided enhance the understanding of how the program is performing and enable prognosis of future performance. For more information on the relationship between portfolio, program, project, and operations management, refer to Section 1.2.3 in the *PMBOK® Guide*.

1.5.2 USE OF EVM FOR MANAGING PERFORMANCE DURING THE WHOLE PORTFOLIO, PROGRAM, AND PROJECT LIFE CYCLES

The primary reason for making business investments is to deliver the benefits that generate strategic competitive advantage and addition of business value. This requires the alignment of organizational change initiatives—primarily programs and projects—with organizational strategy. Effective alignment requires the application of disciplined portfolio management and includes benefits realization management. Most enterprises need to strengthen their benefits realization practices. Benefits realization needs to be measured in a way that is compatible with current EVM principles and practices so that EV concepts may be applied at the program and portfolio levels. The basic principle of EV starts with the establishment of a PMB and the measurement of progress against it. For EV to be applied, both governance and management at the program and portfolio levels should agree to establish a PMB for either the program or the portfolio.

EVM methodology was developed to measure scope accomplishment plus cost and schedule performance. The term EV can be thought of as scope accomplishment—the accomplished or realized part of the project scope. However, when referring to attaining overall organizational value or the addition of value, the application of EV principles and concepts may be modified to address benefits realization from the outputs and outcomes of component programs and projects. Benefits realization leads to the resulting addition of value for the whole organization through effective portfolio, program, and project management. EVM is an excellent methodology to adapt and apply within the organization to measure the performance of programs based on benefits realization and the performance of portfolios based on the creation of additional value for the organization. EVM principles and concepts may be applied to determine portfolio or program performance, as follows:

◆ For the determination of the overall achievement of desired resulting portfolio value (economic or other) based on aggregate portfolio component performance metrics, and

◆ For the determination of the overall achievement of the planned performance for the portfolio or program measured for the whole system and not cumulatively for each component. The metric becomes a measurement of added value for portfolios and a measurement of benefits realization for programs.

EV principles and good project management practices may be applied at the portfolio and program levels in two distinct ways.

◆ **EVM applied toward measuring the performance of each individual program or portfolio component.** This includes performance analysis results for each component that are consolidated and integrated toward the development of benefits-based performance metrics for the whole program or portfolio. Performance analysis results include the aggregation of component metrics for the whole portfolio or program. Weighting factors (for relative importance) may be required to be applied to the performance results for each component and each outcome.

◆ **EVM implemented toward measuring the overall, integrated performance of the whole program or portfolio.** This concept implies the development of an appropriate, realistic, time-phased metric to set a benefits-focused baseline and measure delivery and variance from this baseline. Such a baseline should include total cost, time, and benefits accomplishment for program management. The third parameter of EVM (scope) changes to economic (or other) value-add when applying EVM concepts for portfolios. The precondition for developing a realistic baseline plus a monitoring and prediction model is awareness and, when possible, accounting of nonlinear phenomena, such as effects of component interdependencies, uncertainty, and emergent phenomena. The model has to be applicable throughout the program or portfolio life cycles. Once a meaningful, realistic, quantifiable, tangible, time-phased interdependency model has been developed, and the appropriate baseline is set, earned value analysis based on benefit or value forecasts, as well as overall metrics and appropriate indices may be designed and implemented.

Program and project reporting are positively associated with portfolio management performance. PMI's *Pulse of the Profession*® report [4] indicates that effective portfolio reporting to executive management is positively correlated with achieving purpose. Practitioners should define and establish a common communication platform for all portfolio components. When applicable, the same metrics—usually using EVM as a primary method—should be used to measure and compare the performance of all components. A periodic review of the portfolio should be conducted using these comparable metrics. The quality and effectiveness of these metrics depend on the maturity of each organization. Performance management also allows for the establishment of organizational routines to ensure project selection and prioritization based on the organization's strategy.

The Standard for Portfolio Management [5] indicates that more than half of the variance in portfolio management efficiency could be explained through single portfolio component factors: goal setting, decision making, and information availability on single programs or projects. The remaining variances can be explained by (a) the efficiency of project portfolio management (the estimation of the degree to which the portfolio has succeeded in fulfilling its objectives of strategic alignment), (b) the balance of resources across its components, and (c) the realization of strategy and financial yield or value maximization. In any situation, earned value analysis, when applied properly and consistently, can prove to be valuable toward efficient portfolio and program management. Individual work for all components and efforts of all components' teams may be monitored. Aggregated earned value analysis results for the entire program or portfolio can also be tracked and recorded.

Care should be exercised at all levels, but particularly at the portfolio level where the business value of the various portfolio components is discussed. An example of this is when EVM indicates that partial deliveries add value, yet the practitioner does not account for the commercial reality that requires completed deliverables. This means that complete deliverables are required before any assessment of benefits realization can be made. However, even in these cases, there are advantages to being able to have a consistent measure of portfolio component progress and product completeness. For certain portfolio components, this may not be realistic (e.g., interdependencies that produce nonlinear cause and effect relationships). In these cases, there is considerable uncertainty in the value of such WPs, and EVM may need to measure something other than product completeness or activities performed. Under these conditions, activities are not so easily understood and measured to be complete, and a product-based baseline may be more appropriate. In principle, a product is either completed and quality approved or it is not. Moreover, integrating aggregated performance results obtained through EVM at the portfolio or program levels gives information on current status toward the achievement of strategic objectives. The application of EVM concepts at the portfolio and program levels is further discussed in Appendix X3 of this standard.

1.6 BENEFITS OF THE APPLICATION OF EVM

The following are some of the benefits of EVM:

◆ **EVM is a methodology that integrates the measurement of scope, cost, and schedule** (see also Section 1.3). It enables early detection of performance issues, it is used as a tool for risk monitoring and controlling, it allows corrective actions to be implemented in a timely manner, and it enhances the efficiency of the entire project management process.

◆ **EVM uses the segmentation of projects to communicate to stakeholders and to keep the project team focused on progress toward objectives.** In the last few decades, there has been a noticeable growth of EVM as a good practice for performance management in both the public and the private sectors in many countries. EVM contributions and cost effectiveness are widely recognized by many practitioners who appreciate EVM's contribution in providing early warning signs, helping to achieve cost goals, improving communication with and engaging stakeholders, helping to achieve schedule goals, improving scope management, and providing early successes.

◆ **EVM measures performance and enables forecasting of the total project outcomes.** When significant variances occur, they should be analyzed through root cause analysis (RCA) or other data analysis methods, to identify the sources of problems so that corrective actions can be determined.

◆ **EVM also enables the early warning of performance issues, which leads to timely corrective or preventive actions.** Effective EVM relies heavily on careful scope management, including change control, an accurate and reliable budget, precise and regular measurement of work performed plus actual costs incurred within the reporting period, and a realistic schedule. Otherwise, schedule and cost indicators may become misleading and result in suboptimal management decisions and/or unnecessary courses of action. EVM is a system of aligned and correlated project management practices that spans all phases from initiation to planning to execution, to control, and to delivery. EVM aligns and integrates these management functions into a single system and requires that project teams work on the same measurement basis for accurate, timely, and consistent measurement of project performance.

◆ **EVM is useful for the successful management of all change initiatives at any management level (portfolio, program, or project).** Provided that the quality of the data is monitored and controlled, EVM enables data-based decision making. EVM principles are used for reliable monitoring of investments by measuring the consumption of allocated organizational resources. This measurement is the progress of the execution of scope at the specified quality by tracking completion rates, time variances, and so forth.

◆ **EVM allows for a performance comparison among portfolio or program components.** In all cases and at any level (portfolio, program, or project), all measurements are made from a predefined baseline. Naturally, baselines differ according to measurement parameters and objectives. For example, a portfolio accomplishment baseline may be used to report whether the whole portfolio is (a) delivering its overall intended scope in alignment with the overall portfolio budget and (b) creating the envisioned addition of value for the organization. Practitioners can calculate performance indexes that assist in monitoring actual progress results against the corresponding baseline at any time during implementation. For example:

- The number of financial resources that have been consumed given the overall work performed;
- How much scope should have been accomplished given the time elapsed;
- How much time should have passed given the work performed; and
- What would be the best trade-off to address time and/or cost variances at a given point in time.

There is an increasing awareness that, with the challenge in today's competitive environment, organizations should change the way they work to not only remain relevant in the market place, but to also survive. For example, agile approaches may use different performance metrics to focus on budgetary performance with a focus on sustainable steady rates. Project governance depends on reliable and periodic report submittals to track and predict schedule and cost performance throughout the project life cycle. EVM adapted for agile approaches provides performance metrics based on the value of the completed work at any given time and provides forecasts of future progress based on past work in an agile environment.

Organizational agility is much more than simply being responsive. It encompasses the ability to continually adjust and be versatile, changing to meet rapidly altering conditions. In project management, agile is an adaptive approach that typically employs short cycles called timeboxes, which are usually 1–4 weeks in duration. Timeboxes, also known as iterations or sprints, are used to undertake and deliver work, review the results, and adapt as necessary. Timeboxes provide rapid feedback from the customer or end user on approaches and the suitability or acceptability of deliverables. The focus is on realization of interim benefits rather than the completion of activities.

In agile terms, an agile team is a self-organizing, cross-functional team that produces work products and/or deliverables, based on requirements that are expressed as desired features by the product owner. Features are elaborated into a few structured sentences called a user story. Breaking down features into user stories can be helpful for the team because it speaks from the voice of the customer. User stories often belong to a larger defined set of user stories for an iteration with multiple iterations that make up a release.

It is possible to implement EVM in an agile environment using only three basic parameters: backlog, velocity per completed iteration, and cost. For most projects, the concept of release can help define scope and estimate the PV.

1.7 CONDITIONS NECESSARY FOR SUCCESSFUL EVM IMPLEMENTATION

A supportive culture and a knowledgeable organizational environment are critical for a successful EVM implementation. Enterprise environmental factors (EEFs), such as senior management support, the buy-in of project staff, training, organizational culture and leadership, and maturity of the project management system may prove critical toward the successful implementation of an EVMS. A supportive organizational environment consists of a visionary senior management team that provides necessary resources and authority, as well as a knowledgeable project team that is motivated and committed. At the project level, EVM measures outputs. When applied properly at the portfolio level, EVM measures overall portfolio performance, provides a sound forecast for future outcomes, highlights potential risks, and guides present-time corrective actions.

The principles described in Section 1.1 underpin this standard. These principles are intended to incorporate the best EVM concepts and practices into high-level, results-oriented guidance without being too prescriptive by mandating detailed system implementation. It is best applied under a systems approach throughout the portfolio, program, and project management life cycle. To provide for an enduring application, an EVMS deployment should also take into consideration the cultural acceptance of the system within the management framework of the organization.

An EVMS is an important organizational process asset (OPA). The whole EVM process should be planned, preferably at a business unit level and above, before individual project baselines (or portfolio or program individual components) are set. A project management office (PMO) helps to maintain and provide support for this OPA. The actual EVMS should be described and developed (e.g., manual system; automated tool; EVMS linkage to accounting, auditing, procurement, quality management). This approach best delivers the business benefits expected and ensures a continuing return on the investment applied to all organizational endeavors and change initiatives. Practitioners may produce synergistic benefits by having a combined approach toward EVM and risk management. EVM enables forecasting of future performance by extrapolating processed data from the past. Risk management may give a forward view by scanning the future to identify potential dangers to be avoided while simultaneously seeking additional benefits to be captured. An integrated approach using insights from the one methodology to inform the application of the other enables an enhanced analysis leading to more realistic assessments, thus improving the process of correct decision making.

2

INITIATING

The Initiating Process Group consists of those processes performed to define a new project or a new phase of an existing project by obtaining authorization to start the project or phase of a project. Initiating the project includes developing the project charter and identifying all project stakeholders—and their individual needs for timely, accurate information on the scope, cost, and schedule performance of the project.

2.1 OVERVIEW

In order to plan, execute, monitor, control, and close out a project effectively, there should be a clear description and understanding of the project scope. The project charter, using stakeholder needs and high-level project requirements, organizational process assets (OPAs), enterprise environmental factors (EEFs), and customer agreements (when appropriate) is the foundation for defining and elaborating the project scope/project objectives. The scope statement is used by various *PMBOK® Guide* processes to fully plan the project.

The purpose of the Initiating processes is to align the stakeholders' expectations and the project purpose, inform stakeholders of the scope and objectives, and discuss how their participation in the project and its associated phases can help to ensure their expectations are met.

The Initiating Process Group formally establishes a new project or a new phase of an existing project, and, if not already assigned, the project manager is appointed and authorized to apply resources to project activities. The project sponsor and the project manager, if assigned, initiate the project by generating the project charter document. The project charter provides the high-level project requirements, including the potential application and tailoring of an earned value management system (EVMS).

Initiating the project includes identifying project stakeholders and their individual requirements for timely and accurate information on the scope, cost, and schedule performance of the project. The application of earned value management (EVM) on a project can vary widely depending on the stakeholder requirements, project performance management needs for monitoring requirements, legal or contract requirements, and organizational/customer reporting requirements. The application of EVM also depends on the organization culture and organization maturity.

There are many considerations that should be taken into account when deciding to implement an EVMS. The project risk level and the organization's willingness for taking risks can drive the need for enhanced management methods. Tailoring the EVMS to the project needs, organizational requirements, and environment is an important consideration for an effective lean implementation that provides useful data to the project team and stakeholders, supporting their decision making during project execution.

2.2 CONSIDERATIONS FOR THE PROJECT CHARTER

The project charter is a document approved and usually issued by an entity external to the project, such as a sponsor, program or project management office (PMO), or portfolio governing body chairperson or authorized representative external to the project, who formally authorizes the existence of a project and provides the assigned project manager with the required authority to apply resources to project activities. The project charter establishes a partnership between the performing organization and the requesting organization or customer. In addition to the elements currently listed in the *PMBOK® Guide* project charter, the following EVM-related questions should be considered:

◆ Is an integrated scope, schedule, and cost measurement needed to track project performance?

◆ Does the organization or customer require EVM methods to be applied?

◆ Does the project include agile delivery methods for some or all components?

◆ Do project complexities drive enhanced performance measurement?

◆ Do perceived risks drive the need for enhanced performance management?

◆ Are performance metrics required by financing institutions or other stakeholders?

◆ Are there any constraints/assumptions in applying EVM methods?

◆ Does the project have an adaptive life cycle that requires continuous enhancement to the performance management baseline?

When the project manager and stakeholders choose to implement an EVM approach as a requirement for project planning, executing, monitoring and controlling, and closing, this requirement should be documented in the project charter. The project manager can also decide to use EVM as an enhanced management approach when it is not included in the project charter as a requirement.

For most projects, when the use of EVM is established by the sponsor/project manager during project initiation, it is recommended that the project charter also include:

◆ Overall approach to implement the EVM system (EVMS) (e.g., tailored versus existing OPA);

◆ Key stakeholders involved in the implementation of the EVMS and their key roles and responsibilities;

◆ Budget and other resources available to implement the EVMS (if available);

◆ Management requirements that the EVMS will address (e.g., agile delivery methods, types of reports, management questions, and analysis it will produce and deliver); and

◆ Expected benefits of implementing the EVMS (see Section 1).

An EVMS can be implemented in various forms, ranging from the simple to very elaborate depending upon the nature and type of project. In the Initiating processes, the level of complexity and effort required to be implemented and used should be commensurate with the project's importance and management complexity. This balance is documented in the project charter.

After the project charter is approved, the high-level requirements are further decomposed and documented. Stakeholder needs are refined into documented project requirements and product and/or service requirements in a project management plan. The project requirements documentation should include considerations for implementing EVM as a project management requirement and deliverable of the project (see Section 3).

2.3 CONSIDERATIONS FOR STAKEHOLDERS

Identifying stakeholders should be done regularly throughout the project and includes analyzing and documenting their interests, involvement, interdependencies, influence, and potential impact on success of the project. The application of EVM on a project can vary depending on the stakeholder requirements, project management performance monitoring requirements, and customer reporting requirements.

Stakeholder engagement strategy is designed to engage the project stakeholders in the success of the project. In order to increase support for the project, areas of interest, type, and degree of influence on the project should be captured for each stakeholder in the stakeholder engagement strategy as part of the project management plan described in Section 1.4.

Stakeholders should consider the implementation of EVM as a beneficial and enhanced performance management framework. The stakeholders, along with the project team, should assess the cost/benefit of implementing EVM on their project. A few strategies to engage stakeholders are:

◆ Schedule regular program status meetings with all stakeholders.

◆ Use an integrated milestone schedule to drive meetings.

◆ Map the earned value (EV) specific indicators to the stakeholders' areas of concern.

◆ Review issues, risks, and milestones.

◆ Send meeting summary, status, progress percentage, issues, action plan, recommendations, change requests, and performance summary to all stakeholders.

◆ When applicable, invite all program stakeholders to agile reviews, demonstrations, and retrospectives.

EVM provides useful management information to stakeholders with key information on the scope/cost/time performance of a project. Stakeholders should be careful not to consider the EVMS as an accounting tool. EVMS can be linked to account planning and actual data but should not be considered an accounting tool. Care should be taken not to overburden the EVMS with too many rules from other systems, such as accounting, material management, contract management, and so forth. EVM is a management tool designed to support real-time and forward-looking decision making, as opposed to a retrospective accounting tool. The level and type of information needed about a project's status may vary greatly from one stakeholder to another. The client, owner, or senior management may simply need a summary-level highlight report that indicates whether a project is on time and within budget. By contrast, the project manager needs more detail in order to make timely and effective decisions when managing project performance.

Several reporting methods have evolved for presenting EVM analysis data and information. These methods are designed to address diverse stakeholder needs and should be identified during project initiation and documented in both the project charter and later in the project management plan. Several of these methods may be used on a given project to meet the needs of different stakeholder audiences. Further descriptions of the reporting methods are included in Section 4.

An EVMS generates a significant amount of data and metrics that are timely, reliable, and useful to management for decision-making purposes. Its primary goal is to provide information to all project stakeholders, both those working on the project team and those outside of the project. This information can be used to monitor the project status, understand the causes of variation, make decisions, and communicate project performance to others. At the same time, this information can be used to align expectations and build consensus for the best options for the project. This information not only includes current project conditions and past performance, but also includes forecasts of the project's future performance trends and what-if scenarios, which are most valuable and critical in project management decision making.

2.4 DETERMINING THE APPLICABILITY OF THE EVM SYSTEM (EVMS)

2.4.1 INTRODUCTION

An EVM system (EVMS) is a system of principles, methods, and processes that integrates with tools and people to assess performance of integrated portfolio, program, or project management as described in Section 1. Tailoring the EVMS to meet stakeholders' needs is a consideration in project initiation as described below. EVM can be as simple as an integration of the *PMBOK® Guide* processes with the addition of EV techniques. It can be an enhanced, disciplined framework used within a system for the purpose of managing a project that integrates scope, cost, and schedule time-phased baselines with established performance measures. Often the EVMS is integrated with other organizational needs and is described as an enterprise-level EVMS description that governs the use of the framework. It also describes the processes, practices, techniques, procedures, rules, and tools to be implemented in a project. A project team may also consider tailoring the framework by considering lean principles to meet project and stakeholder needs.

An organizational EVMS typically codifies EEFs, such as organizational culture and governance, information technology tools, legal restrictions, customer requirements, and so forth, into a system description. Other procedures are incorporated as OPAs, which are usually implemented within a project management set of processes/system. Depending on the EEFs, the project team can usually tailor the implementation of the organizational EVMS to the needs of the project. Not all elements of an EVMS need to be implemented on a project for EVM to be an effective management tool, as implementations can be simple or elaborate.

2.4.2 CONSIDERATIONS FOR IMPLEMENTATION OF EVMS

During project initiation, a decision is made as to whether an EVMS will be used for the project and, if so, to what extent. EVMS comprises the additional work that includes development of processes, definitions of stakeholders' roles and responsibilities, and the supporting IT infrastructure. The implementation of an EVMS becomes part of the project scope as a deliverable, and it is incorporated into the project management plan and the WBS scope description/dictionary. Another approach is to consider the implementation of an EVMS as a separate project that is connected with the current project.

During project initiation, it is important to assess additional benefits/considerations for other functions/organizations within the company to use an EVMS, including:

◆ Is the project considered to be a complex/high-risk project?

◆ Is EV mandated by the sponsor or company policy or improvement action initiated by the project/program/ portfolio manager?

◆ Is accurate, timely, and reliable reporting to stakeholders a key success factor?

Additional questions to consider when making the decision to implement EVMS that result from consideration of EEFs and/or OPAs are:

◆ Can you provide reliable data for your project status?

◆ If you use EVM, how mature is the organization that is applying EVM?

◆ Is it used in all the projects in the organization or only in some areas?

◆ Do people at all levels understand the concepts that EVM uses?

◆ Does your organization typically use EVM? If not, what obstacles does that pose?

◆ Does your organization's project governance model already incorporate EVM?

◆ Are there manual or software methods defined for your organization's use of EVM?

◆ Are there subject matter experts (SMEs) available to assist with the development and use of EVM?

◆ Does the contract (if applicable) mandate EVM?

◆ Are there plans, policies, or procedures for performing EVM in your organization?

◆ Are there lessons learned available in the organization's knowledge management database/repository related to EVM?

◆ Are there directives regarding EVM from the enterprise PMO?

◆ Is there a project management information system (PMIS) used by the organization?

◆ Are there templates to aid in the use of EVM?

◆ Do the sponsor and other key stakeholders understand EVM?

◆ Do the accounting personnel understand EVM?

◆ If no OPAs are available to implement EVM on your projects, are there sufficient resources and budget to develop the required project processes to implement EVM?

◆ If EVM is not used to manage project performance, what will the project manager and project team use to manage project performance?

◆ Are there project constraints (schedule, cost, scope, quality, benefits, and/or risk) that are influencing the decision to use EVM?

◆ Do the EEFs and OPAs include tailored approaches for the agile/hybrid components of the project?

◆ Are partner organizations and subcontractors ready to systematically provide data required to support EVM?

◆ What are the requirements of the financing organizations and other stakeholders regarding performance reporting?

A consolidated set of OPAs into an EVMS description is not required but might be advantageous when an organization intends to implement EVM systematically across its portfolio of projects. The EVMS to be used should be described in the project management plan as outlined in Section 3.2. Specific needs to be considered when planning an EVM system include:

◆ Tailoring of an existing organizational EVMS (OPAs) in coordination with the process owner, if applicable;

◆ Tailoring/interface with organizations and/or customer PMIS; and

◆ Standardization of indexes, thresholds, documentation, and reporting.

The project management plan should address the extent to which the project will use OPAs and EEFs, and how the system will affect the integrated management approach. Whereas other project management Knowledge Areas or supporting activities may be managed by a specialist, the accountability of integration management should not be delegated or transferred. The project manager has the overall responsibility for the execution of the project and should lead the design and implementation of the EVM framework on the project. A management tool is aimed at helping managers to make better decisions without eliminating accountability.

2.4.3 TAILORING OF EVM

Once the implementation of EVM is established, it may be tailored for use on projects based on complexity, risk, and other factors as outlined in this section. The application of EVMS descriptions and OPAs should be tailored based on stakeholder requirements, project risks, project funding, project importance, complexity, and other considerations. The stakeholders and project team should provide input when determining whether to implement EVM on a project. Examples of tailoring EVM include:

◆ Defining and having to track various items in the baseline, such as undistributed budget and authorized unpriced work;

◆ Reporting variances on a cumulative basis only or to a specified level of the work breadkdown structure (WBS);

◆ Requiring varying threshold levels for variance reporting;

◆ Using EVM only on some specific scope components;

◆ Revising the level of suppliers' and contractors' involvement;

- Using available information from existing data sources such as financial systems, project management systems, and time-tracking systems; and

- Using a governance approach structured to meet the organization's objectives, yet being flexible enough to implement an agile/hybrid project.

The decision to tailor an EVM approach should be made during the initiating phase, described in the project charter prior to the planning phase (see Section 3), and finalized during the planning phase.

2.4.4 DEPLOYMENT OF EVMS

The deployment of an organization-wide EVMS can be approached as a separate project with the full complement of project attributes. When developed within a specific project, the project may become a subproject or a scope component of it. To be successful, the EVMS deployment should be managed under a project management process. Consideration should be given to the following areas:

- Organizations should decide if they will:

  - Blend the additional earned value framework needs into existing process documents,

  - Write completely new and separate process documents, or construct a combination of both.

- Since EVMS is a distributed, collaborative, inclusive (integrated) management system, its principles should be understood and embraced by all project management personnel and decision leaders through effective training and mentoring.

- Sponsorship toward the application of EVM should be provided by project governance.

- Most commercially available project management software contains an EV module with varying levels of scope, cost, and schedule collection required. The need for new performance management tools and their integration with the legacy infrastructure within an organization should be addressed along with the development of data process flow between systems.

- High-level requirements should:

  - Include an analysis of the project complexity and stakeholder needs,

  - Include the organizational systems to establish governance structure for managing program and project risks across all teams, and

  - Ensure governance structure is tailored to be consistent with the project requirements, including stakeholder needs.

Each of these areas above should be addressed during planning and implementation. The degree to which each item is addressed is entirely based upon the effective tailoring of the system to suit each organization's and project's specific performance management environment, objectives, and goals. From the start of the project, during initiation and planning, care should be taken to align the EVM requirements to the individual situation. Later, continued functionality and benefits should be verified as the system is deployed and used during project execution. Continuous improvement of the EVMS should be pursued actively by the project team throughout the project (see also Section 4.7). During closing, as described in Section 5, both a lessons-learned exercise and knowledge management activities are conducted to ensure the improvement of the EVMS for the subsequent project phases and future projects.

Once EVM is implemented, the use of information related to scope, schedule, and cost is made available for project performance analysis. This provides the leadership with valid, timely forecasts and feedback to guide portfolio, program, and project management decision making toward success.

3

PLANNING THE PROJECT

The Planning Process Group consists of those processes that establish the total scope of the effort, define and refine the objectives, and develop the course of action required to attain those objectives.

3.1 OVERVIEW

The Planning Process Group is key to the implementation of projects and the implementation of EVM. Because EVM is an integrating methodology, it requires an enhanced project management approach. When using EVM, the project team should spend time planning the project early in the project life cycle to take advantage of the integrating methodology for performance management. The team likely needs to return to the Planning processes as the team executes the project to either: (a) continue planning through the project life cycle using the rolling wave approach or (b) continue on the current plan executing the projects based on decisions made relative to baseline changes. It is important to allow the enhanced integrated discipline EVM provides to help the project team proactively manage the project for a better outcome.

The key to getting value out of EVM is to implement forward-looking, enhanced planning early in the project, which is informed by using past performance to adjust the future plans forecast with a revised estimate to complete (ETC)[1] (see also Section 4).

Successful EVM relies on the performance of project management fundamentals. Therefore, the assumption in this standard is that, consistent with the *PMBOK® Guide,* the processes falling within the Planning Process Group are being used in an integrated manner with an enhanced level of discipline that reflects the desires of the project team and other stakeholders. This section outlines how the various Planning processes are affected by the implementation of EVM. In most cases, there are no significant additions, but there is a requirement for integration.

The application of a tailored approach along with any other additional requirements for an EVM implementation should have been captured in the Initiating processes and included in a signed project charter (see Section 2).

---

[1] This same principle is used by the methodology known as reference class forecasting, which is mostly used during the planning of large programs as well as for megaprojects.

3.1.1 PLANNING FOR PROJECTS THAT USE EARNED VALUE MANAGEMENT (EVM)

When planning a project using EVM methodology, the Planning Process Group is best approached as follows: develop plans, develop and integrate baselines, and establish the performance measurement baseline (PMB) (see Figure 3-1). The EVM methodology, per the EVM principles noted in Section 1, requires the implementation of a disciplined project management method with enhanced focus on integration. The enterprise environmental factors (EEFs) and organizational process assets (OPAs), as described in Section 2.1, should determine the level of discipline and integration, relative to any specific earned value management system (EVMS) being used by the project.

The remainder of this section addresses the following Planning Process Group activities:

◆ Developing the project management plan (Section 3.2);

◆ Developing data and integrating the scope, schedule, and cost baselines considering resources and risks (Section 3.3);

◆ Setting the performance measurement baseline (Section 3.4); and

◆ Applying EVM in an agile/hybrid environment (Section 3.5).

Figure 3-1 depicts the process flow diagram for the Planning Process Group when implementing EVM. The numbers provided are the specific sections from the *PMBOK® Guide*.

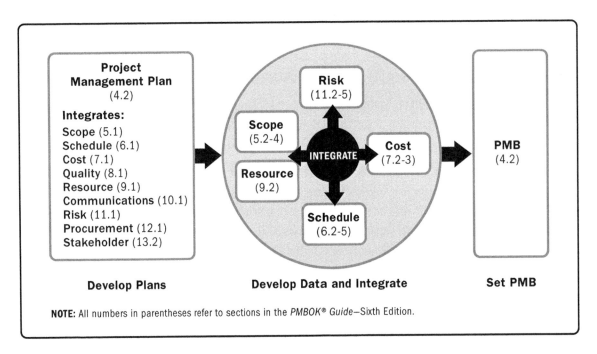

Figure 3-1. Planning Earned Value: Process Flow Diagram

3.1.2 CONSIDERATIONS FOR PLANNING THE USE OF EVM

Whether the decision to use EVM is made during the project's Initiating processes or when organizing and preparing the life cycle phases, several considerations for planning are key to a successful implementation of EVM on a project. Typically, during project initiation, the project charter (see Section 2) and discussions with project stakeholders address whether the use of EVM as a performance management methodology is beneficial for the project. However, the project team can also decide whether the use of EVM would be beneficial and how much of the method should be used. Whether required or not, the project team should determine whether EVM adds value to the project management approach, just as a team decides on which of the processes within the *PMBOK® Guide* they want to implement. The number of process interactions and interdependencies between processes varies, based on the needs of the project.

Planning processes generally fall into one of three categories:

◆ **Processes used once or at predefined points in the project.** The Plan Procurement Management process may be implemented at a predefined point during the project planning and not repeated.

◆ **Processes that are performed periodically as needed.** The Acquire Resources process is performed as a project progresses and when resource needs change.

◆ **Processes that are performed continuously throughout the project.** The Define Activities process may occur throughout the project life cycle, especially when the project uses rolling wave planning or an adaptive development approach.

For EVM, all three categories of processes come into play. Processes that are performed periodically or continuously are applied more frequently when the project uses a rolling wave planning approach. EVM does not require new Knowledge Areas or specific processes beyond the *PMBOK® Guide*, but it does require an increased level of integration and discipline in addition to the expansion of a few project processes (e.g., earned value [EV] techniques, time-phasing budget). It can be advantageous to use a rolling wave approach, which lessens the impacts of having to integrate all scope, cost, and schedule baselines with EV techniques up front.

The key to the successful use of EVM is having a well-designed work breakdown structure (WBS) with a clear structure for defining control accounts (CAs), work packages (WPs), and activities. According to the *PMBOK® Guide*, a CA is a management control point where scope, budget, actual cost, and schedule are integrated and compared to the EV for performance measurement. A CA has one or more work and/or planning packages; each package belongs to a single CA. The scope is decomposed into components through the use of CAs and WPs. For EVM, this structure—a breakout of WBS and organizational breakdown structure (OBS)—becomes the key management control points at which the scope, budget, and schedule are integrated, baselined, and compared for performance measurements. Understanding the logic/schema for the CA/WP breakout is a key planning activity that crosses Knowledge Areas, as the CAs and WPs are the points in which the Knowledge Area processes are integrated.

Not all control accounts need to have EV applied, because the use of EVM does not need to be an all-or-nothing decision at the project level. A low-risk CA or set of CAs, which might be outsourced under a fixed-price procurement effort, could be excluded from the PMB. During planning, the team needs to decide the extent to which EVM will be applied given the CA for the project.

3.2 DEVELOPING THE PROJECT MANAGEMENT PLAN

Develop Project Management Plan is the process of defining, preparing, and coordinating all plan components and consolidating them into an integrated project management plan (see Section 4.2 of the *PMBOK® Guide*). Planning for EVM follows the same process while following the EVM principles outlined in Section 1. Those principles drive one important requirement, which is the use of EVM techniques (see Section 3.2.2.2) for implementing performance management and oversight by enabling discipline and integration.

The *PMBOK® Guide* (See Section 4.2.3.1) notes that the project management plan integrates and consolidates all of the subsidiary plans and baselines, and other essential information for managing the project. When using EVM methodology, an integrated project management plan should address the specific needs of EVM within each of the 19 project management plan components described in *PMBOK® Guide* and shown in the list below. These include:

- ◆ **Subsidiary plans.** The 10 subsidiary plans also need to address, as appropriate, the EVM methodology as it applies to the project. The subsidiary plans are:

  - Scope management plan,
  - Requirements management plan,
  - Schedule management plan,
  - Cost management plan,
  - Quality management plan,
  - Resource management plan,
  - Communications management plan,
  - Risk management plan,
  - Procurement management plan, and
  - Stakeholder engagement plan.

◆ **Baselines.** The three baselines need to be addressed as they are integrated into the PMB. The baselines are:

- Scope baseline (see Section 5.4.3.1 of the *PMBOK® Guide*),

- Schedule baseline (see Section 6.5.3.1 of the *PMBOK® Guide*), and

- Cost baseline (see Section 7.3.3.1 of the *PMBOK® Guide*).

◆ **Additional components.** These five components also need to address, as appropriate, the PMB when implementing EVM. The components are:

- Change management plan,

- Configuration management plan,

- Project life cycle description,

- Development approach, and

- Management reviews.

Note that there may also be agreements with other parts of the performing or sponsoring organization outside of the project to define the required information flow for EVM when they are not covered in existing OPAs that define the organization's implementation of EVM.

3.2.1 SCOPE PLANNING

Specific needs to be considered when planning for EVM:

◆ **General.** All *PMBOK® Guide* Project Scope Management processes are used within EVM.

◆ **Work breakdown structure (WBS).** The WBS is key. The WBS is used as the single structure that integrates the scope, schedule, and cost baselines together at a common level. The WBS decomposes the scope of work to be carried out by the project team, and a WBS dictionary defines the scope of work for each WBS component.

◆ **Control account (CA).** A management control point where scope, budget, actual cost, and schedule are integrated and compared to EV for performance measurement. A CA has work and planning packages.

◆ **Work package (WP).** The work defined at the lowest level of the WBS for which cost and duration are estimated and managed. Work packages usually have an identifier. These identifiers provide a structure for hierarchical summation of cost, schedule, and resource information and form a code of accounts. Each WP is part of a control account.

◆ **Planning package.** The work defined at a WBS component below the CA for which cost and duration are estimated, but has not been broken out for measurement.

3.2.2 SCHEDULE PLANNING

All *PMBOK® Guide* Project Schedule Management processes are used within EVM with the addition of adopting rules for performance management. The rules noted are included in Section 3.2.2.2.

3.2.2.1 CONSIDERATIONS FOR SCHEDULE PLANNING

Additional considerations for schedule planning are:

◆ Set a performance measurement baseline by planning the total effort needed. Detailed planning does not need to be accomplished for the whole project at the start of the project. Place future efforts in the control account and plan the details at some future point in time using rolling wave planning. When using a rolling wave planning approach, develop a rolling wave plan to align the rolling waves with project milestones. Then by using planning packages initially, use summary-level schedule activities that align with CAs to plan for work between project milestones in the future. Plan work in detail prior to execution within the applicable rolling wave period.

Rolling wave planning is an interactive planning technique in which the work to be accomplished in the near term is planned in detail, while future work is planned at a higher level. The project team usually waits until the project component or subcomponent is defined and its requirements are approved. Once this is accomplished, the project team begins the detail planning for WBS/CA for this part of the project. The rolling wave approach allows for the enhanced level of integration to be accomplished at manageable intervals. Note that future parts of CAs that are not detail planned in WPs are included in planning packages. Planning packages do not need to include EV techniques, but need to be further broken out into WPs before the work is started. This is often accomplished by the project team during detail planning for the next rolling wave, but only needs to be accomplished before the work begins to allow a planning package to be converted into work packages. The project team may also follow established procedures (organizational process assets).

◆ Define project-specific rules, such as level of accuracy, units of measure (hours, days, and weeks), control thresholds, reporting format, and so on, to support EVM implementations.

◆ Specify rules of performance measurement that are consistent with scope and cost planning (see Sections 3.2.2.1 and 3.2.3).

◆ Develop the rules for estimating the duration and establishing schedule, including the level of detail (basis of estimate) and how risk and uncertainty will be incorporated and/or characterized in the schedule.

◆ Address the integration of the scheduling software within the overall project management information system (PMIS).

3.2.2.2 RULES OF PERFORMANCE MEASUREMENT CRITERIA

Determine the measurement method, technique, or criteria to be used for progress evaluation of the activity types within a WP. During the planning process, the project manager and those managing the CAs determine an approach for measuring the scope accomplishment for each CA. The scope is typically measured at the work package level, but can be measured at the activity level.

EV is a measure of the work performed based on a formula, taking into account the budgeted and actual cost or other unit of measure of that work at a given point in time. The method for measuring work performed is selected during project planning prior to commencing the work, and is the basis for performance measurement during project execution. In this standard, all costs are provided in U.S. dollars.

Organizations may have explicit guidelines or processes for selecting measurement methods. The guidelines should include method selection, measurement accuracy, measurement period, measurement unit, data collection, and reporting. Choosing an inappropriate performance measurement method may result in misleading status, and subsequently result in nonconstructive or ineffective management action.

The primary goal in choosing a performance measurement method is to have the most objective, accurate, and timely assessment that is appropriate for the project work, schedule, and cost status. Each work package has its own unique characteristics; therefore, there is not one single best way to measure progress. To accommodate the different types of work, there are several accepted methods to measure work performance. The EV methods are generally assigned and applied to activities within a work package.

There are three classes of work: (a) discrete effort (e.g., measurable work), (b) apportioned effort (e.g., work that is factored to measurable work), and (c) level of effort (LOE) (e.g., nonmeasurable work). Each of these classes has one or more measurement methods available, and each method has its own specific characteristics that determine how it is applied to the work. The major drivers to determine the method are duration and tangibility of the deliverables. Table 3-1 includes guidelines for selecting appropriate types of measurement methods. Table 3-2 provides key points to consider when determining the measurement method.

The example in Appendix X4 expands upon the examples in this section.

Table 3-1. Guidelines for Selecting Measurement Method

Type of Work/ Tasks		Characteristics	
		Tangible (Measurable)	Intangible (Nonmeasurable)
Duration	Short (1-2 Periods)	Fixed Formula Apportioned Effort	Level of Effort
	Longer (Exceeds 2 Periods)	Weighted Milestone Percent Complete Physical Measurement	

Table 3-2. Key Points When Determining Measurement Methods

Measurement Methods		Key Points to Consider When Determining the Method
Discrete Effort	Fixed Formula	50/50, 25/75, 0/40/60, etc.—Using this method, work is credited for EV as soon as it starts with a specific percent. (25/75 starts with 25% being taken in the first period in which the method is used with 75% taken when work is completed). Note that the real progress is invisible, and this method can give a false sense of accomplishment. This measurement method should only be used for work that spans two or three reporting periods.
		0/100—The 0/100 method does not incrementally credit EV for partial work; therefore, the start of the work is not explicitly reported. This measurement method should only be used for work that is scheduled to start and complete within one reporting period.
	Weighted Milestone	The weighted milestone method has one or more milestones in the measurement period. Each milestone has an objective, verifiable accomplishment that is associated with it. The milestones are weighted to reflect the relative accomplishment of the milestones against the whole.
	Percent Complete	The percent complete method entails an estimate of the percent complete of the BAC at each measurement point. There should be measurable criteria associated with the percent complete measurements, or they can be subjective and inaccurate.
	Physical Measurement	The evaluation of work progress in the project work packages is related to the physical nature. Whereas testing, measurement procedures, and/or specifications should be explicit and be agreed upon in advance.
Apportioned Effort		To use apportioned effort, the project manager should have pragmatic knowledge and validated performance records to create the percentage of apportioned effort pertaining to the discrete work package.
Level of Effort		Level of effort (LOE) can be misused and distort the real progress of the project, because the PV of the LOE determines EV for each reporting period (there is never a schedule variance) no matter how much of the work is actually performed.

◆ **Discrete effort.** Discrete effort is a tangible, measurable activity that is planned, measured, and yields a specific output. Discrete effort is directly related to specific end products or services with distinct and measurable points. Examples include pouring concrete for a bridge abutment or writing a user's manual.

Four principal measurement methods are available for WPs classified as discrete effort. Measurement methods used for discrete effort enable accurate measurement of work accomplished. The key is to measure the output with reasonable accuracy. Other methods of measure could be possible given the nature of the work; however, the four principal discrete effort measurement methods are:

- Fixed formula,
- Weighted milestone,
- Percent complete, and
- Physical measurement.

◆ **Apportioned effort.** Apportioned effort is used for work with a direct, supportive relationship to discrete work. The value for the support task is determined based on the EV of the referenced base activity. Apportioned effort can include such work as quality assurance, inspection, and testing activities. An apportioned work effort is estimated as a percentage of the referenced discrete work effort. The percent allocation to discrete effort is used when there are sufficient performance records and knowledge of the interrelationship between the apportioned effort and the discrete effort. In Figure 3-2, the discrete effort at the second measurement point is $5,200. The apportioned effort is 10% of the discrete effort. Therefore, the apportioned value at the second measurement point is 10% of $5,200 or $520. The actual discrete effort accomplished at the end of the second period was $7,800; therefore, the apportioned EV at the second measurement point is 10% of $7,800 or $780.

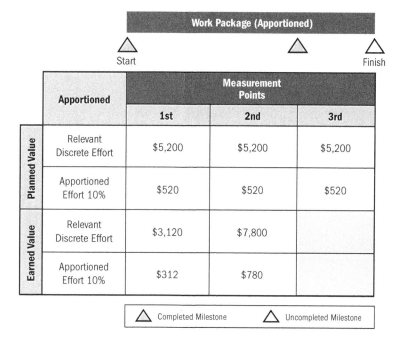

Figure 3-2. Example of Apportioned Effort

◆ **Level of effort (LOE).** Level-of-effort (LOE) activities should be kept to a minimum because the method does not provide an indication of schedule performance. In many cases, the traditional use of LOE on activities could be better measured through apportioned methods. When LOE is used, it should only be used on efforts that do not directly produce definitive end products that can be delivered or measured objectively. The use of LOE means that EV is based on the passage of time and consumed project resources. LOE is not necessarily characterized by a uniform rate of work over a period of time. A planned value (PV) is assigned to each LOE work package for each measurement period. This PV is credited as EV at the end of the measurement period. EV is accrued in line with PV, which means LOE activities do not have a schedule variance. Cost variance (CV) can be incurred, however, because the actual cost (AC) is often not exactly the same as the EV. It is also important to note that LOE activities can accrue EV in the absence of AC. This can happen when work was planned, EV is earned, but no work—therefore no costs—are actually incurred. It is this scenario where LOE is not the preferred method and should be limited or not used at all.

Using the same work package as in Figure 3-2, Figure 3-3 shows where EV is equal to PV at all measurement points. This limits the performance measurement insight from this measurement method for the activity in question.

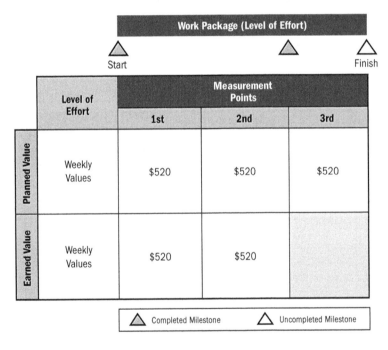

Figure 3-3. Example of Level of Effort (LOE)

3.2.3 COST PLANNING

In the cost planning stage:

◆ All *PMBOK® Guide* Project Cost Management planning processes are used within EVM.

◆ During planning, the project team defines which performance measurement methods are used, including the value, in some unit of measure, typically cost, that will be monitored. Traditionally this has been a time-phased budget expressed in units of some currency (e.g., dollars, euros, yen), but any value measure can be used, such as hours.

◆ The project team adopts rules for estimating costs, including the level of detail. This determines how much detail is captured in the basis of estimate. This is important depending on the measurement method being used. The detail developed and captured in the cost estimate should support the proposed measurement design. The cost estimates and the rationale for them are often captured in a document called the basis of estimate.

◆ The project management plan and procedures provide criteria regarding how risk/uncertainty is incorporated into the estimate and then characterized in the reserves (whether management or contingency). Frequently, EEFs and OPAs provide specific guidance on how risks are incorporated into both the schedule and cost baselines.

◆ Additionally, the project team should time phase the cost in the same manner as the scheduled work is time phased.

3.2.4 RESOURCE PLANNING

In the resource planning phase, it is essential to identify and plan for the appropriate required resources. It is also important for these resources to be available during execution to ensure both timeliness and quality of the data to be collected.

◆ All *PMBOK® Guide* Project Resource Management planning processes are used within EVM.

◆ The project team determines the criteria for the management control points, which are the CAs.

◆ The project team develops a responsibility assignment matrix (RAM) that tracks WBS (scope) to the responsible organization (OBS) in which all work scope and resources or cost under the EVM approach are mapped to control accounts (see also Section 3.3.1). Prior to setting up the RAM, the following structures should be developed:

- Breakdown of the WBS should be to the lowest level at which work will be managed. For some WBS components, such as a subsystem which is being purchased or outsourced, the need for further breakdown is not necessary. Other WBS at the subsystems level may need to be designed and the WBS further decomposed so the design can be managed.

- Level of breakdown for the OBS structure (organizational units, cross-functional teams, or other structure), is the lowest level at which work is managed.

3.2.4.1 CONSIDERATIONS FOR RESOURCE PLANNING

To integrate the scope, schedule, and various baselines, several considerations need to be made before a common integrated structure is established. Such a structure needs to include:

- **Responsibility assignment matrix (RAM).** A grid that shows the project resources assigned to each work package. The RAM shows the integration of the work in the WBS and the resources in the OBS for the purpose of assigning project scope to a person or a team. The RAM delineates levels of control and responsibility and indicates the authority and responsibility levels for the project. The intersection points of the OBS and the WBS are typically the control account. The individual responsible and accountable for the successful delivery of the scope, schedule, and budget in a CA is usually referred to as the manager of the control account or the control account manager. The RAM is further described in Section 3.3.1.

- **CA structure.** A CA is associated with one hierarchical path within the WBS structure and typically one OBS element. It is permissible for multiple organizations (frequently called performing organizations) to work within a team on the scope within a control account, but management responsibility and accountability usually belong to only one organization (the responsible organization).

- **Level of detail.** The project manager should consider the appropriate level of detail for the project. The project manager should recognize the dangers of keeping the level of scope decomposition too high or too low. At too high a level, the size of the CAs (in budget, schedule, and/or scope) may overwhelm the manager of the CAs. At too low a level of the WBS, the sheer number of CAs will be distracting, but more likely detrimental to the successful accomplishment of the work within the parameters of the control account. Additionally, driving the level of the CA down increases the amount of management oversight, the intervention required by stakeholders, and also the cost of the monitoring and control processes and practices. The level of detail also should be managerially consistent with the capability and span of control of the control account manager. The project needs to be staffed with control account managers with the right level of knowledge and experience, otherwise there will be limited value to creating the control account management structure. The control account managers need to receive training and coaching in order to manage the CAs that are appropriate for the project. Ultimately, there needs to be a balance between the needs of the project for performance measurement and the capabilities of the project team and organization.

3.2.5 RISK PLANNING

Important risk planning considerations are:

◆ All *PMBOK® Guide* Project Risk Management planning processes should be used within EVM.

◆ The project team establishes the process for determining how the work for risk responses is included in the baselines.

◆ The project team, often with sponsors, determines the extent to which the contingency reserve and/or management reserve are going to be used and to what extent the baselines are going to be risk based. Data analysis, as described in Sections 6.5.2., 6.6.2.6, 7.2.2.6, 7.4.2.2, and 9.6.2.1 of the *PMBOK® Guide* should be used.

◆ The project team integrates risk management into the development of the risk-based cost and schedule estimates, including quantitative cost and schedule risk analysis.

Risk planning should also address the EEFs around the use of contingency reserve and management reserve. This standard follows the *PMBOK® Guide*, which may not be the environment in which the project will handle risk management and the resulting reserves. It is critical to project success to have realistic expectations about risks that need to be addressed within the project budget. The project team, including those managing at the CA level, can best manage effort with some reserve(s). How that reserve is documented and measured needs to be clear to the project team and the stakeholders. Note, management reserve is often created for management control purposes and is reserved for unforeseen work that is within scope of the project.

3.2.6 OTHER PLANNING (QUALITY, COMMUNICATIONS, PROCUREMENT, AND STAKEHOLDER)

Other considerations regarding planning are as follows:

◆ All *PMBOK® Guide* processes within the Quality, Communications, Procurement, and Stakeholder Management Knowledge Areas are needed to implement EVM. It is essential for a sustainable EVM implementation to be sponsored continuously by project governance.

◆ Quality planning can be key to a successful EVM implementation. Concepts for continuous improvement, management responsibility, policy compliance, and auditing can all come into play in an EVM implementation. EVM can be helpful in project benchmarking. Additionally, the project team should discuss how EVM will handle delivery of products and services that do not meet quality expectations.

◆ The communications planning approach should include the baseline reviews and approvals that are needed and the stakeholders who need them. The reporting requirements (including variance thresholds), level of integrated analysis (such as risk with schedule and costs), and requirements for updated analyses need to be determined. The communications management plan defines thresholds for EV criteria of schedule variance (SV), cost variance (CV), cost performance index (CPI), and schedule performance index (SPI) and notes when stakeholders are informed and by what methods if thresholds are exceeded.

◆ For procurement planning, the project team determines whether to use EVM for any procurements, and if so, specific instructions for the vendor(s) may be required. Considerations for advance payments, retention money for performance bonds, and payments for material on-site along with other procurement terms need to be considered. In addition, the project team determines how the vendors will integrate EVM data into the overall project's EVM data and how performance measurement periods will be aligned. If EVM is flowed down to vendors/subcontractors, then plans should be adjusted to acknowledge the need to develop how Schedule, Cost, Risk, and other Project Management Knowledge Areas are fed from input provided by the vendors/subcontractors.

◆ Planning stakeholder engagement should consider how EVM will affect engagement efforts along with EEFs and OPAs driven by particular stakeholders. The stakeholder engagement plan can address how the EVM implementation will affect engagements, whether formal or informal. Where appropriate, stakeholder engagement activities should be included in the PMB.

3.3 DEVELOPING DATA AND INTEGRATING THE SCOPE, SCHEDULE, AND COST BASELINES CONSIDERING RESOURCES AND RISKS

The development and integration of the scope, schedule, and cost baselines need to be aligned with the plan/criteria outlined in the project management plan and EVM-related OPAs. In most cases, this is an iterative process that extends into the execution phase, especially when rolling wave planning is used. For the portion of the project in which EVM is being implemented, integrated scope, schedule, and cost baselines need to be created, which will form the basis for the PMB.

In creating the performance measurement baseline, five Knowledge Areas (Project Scope Management, Project Schedule Management, Project Cost Management, Project Risk Management, and Project Resource Management) need to be integrated (see Figure 3-1) in such a manner that the scope, schedule, risk, and cost are associated at a common level across the baselines (either CA, WP, or activity) with an established performance measurement method.

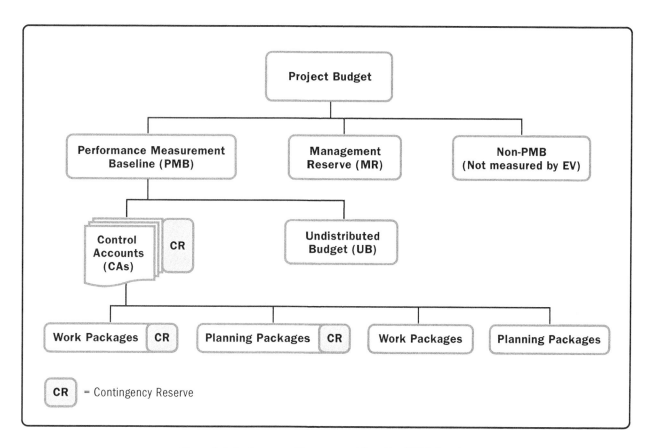

Figure 3-4. Performance Measurement Baseline (PMB) Creation

With the integration of the scope, schedule, and cost baselines, the organization of the project baselines needs to be consistent. This should follow the *PMBOK® Guide* project budget components as outlined in Figure 3-4 (also see the example in Appendix X4). When setting the budget, the project team determines which costs are in and out of the project budget. Cost, such as indirect or overheads, following OPAs and EEFs related to the project, could be excluded. Usually a management reserve (MR) has been determined, which is also typically outside of the cost baseline. The project team also determines whether all or just a portion of the costs will be included in the integrated PMB.

These provide the scope and schedule baselines that are integrated for the PMB. Note that contingency reserves can be allocated at either the control account, work package, or planning package levels. During the planning process, some scope/budget may not yet be distributed to a particular CA, but may be considered as part of the PMB. In this case, the scope and its allocated costs are held in what is often known as undistributed budget (UB). One can look at undistributed budget as a special CA that is holding scope with associated activities and costs that have not been scheduled, therefore are not yet time phased into a planning or work package within a particular CA.

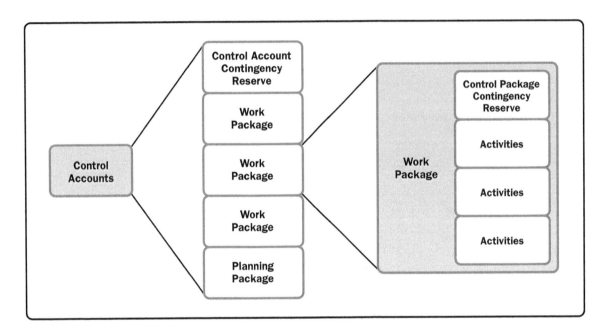

Figure 3-5. Control Account Components

Once the CA structure is set, detailed planning occurs within the CA with work packages, planning packages, and a contingency reserve (see Figure 3-5 and the example in Appendix X4). The project team decides to what level the scope, schedule, and cost baselines will be integrated (i.e., at the CA or work package or activity level). At a minimum, scope, schedule, and cost should be integrated at the CA level, but can be further broken down with the performance measure method applied down to the scope within an activity level along with schedule and costs.

Future scope, especially when a rolling wave concept is being used, can be put into CAs with only planning packages. These future CAs can be a summary of what is eventually broken out into more detailed work packages or possibly a separate CA. (In some industries, the CA that summarizes future work is called a summary-level planning package.) A CA with only a planning package is often used so all project work that will have EVM applied can be planned to some level within the integrated baseline at the start of the project. This collection of near- and future-term CAs forms the PMB.

Sections 3.3.1 through 3.3.5 describe concepts that the project team should consider within each Process Group. Each of these elements need to be integrated to establish the basis for the PMB portion of the project budget.

3.3.1 RESOURCE MANAGEMENT

Resource management is where the level of management effort is determined, which sets the OBS and the structure of responsibility within the RAM. This process sets the management structure by determining the CA structure, which sets the lowest level by which the project will be managed.

3.3.1.1 ASSIGN RESPONSIBILITY WITHIN AN ORGANIZATIONAL BREAKDOWN STRUCTURE (OBS)

Projects can be undertaken within the existing structure of an organization or under a structure tailored for the particular project. Often integrated teams are used, with combined resources from various organizations. Various approaches can be taken depending on the needs of the project and the organizational policies. In either case, the organizational structure for the project itself should reflect the lines of authority and communications within the project. It should also reflect who is responsible for accomplishing the work.

The resulting structure used by the project team becomes the organizational breakdown structure (OBS) used within EVM. The OBS, whether a hierarchical representation of the project organization, an integrated team structure, or some other hybrid structure illustrates the relationship between project activities and the responsible organizational units that perform those activities. The structure relates the control accounts to the organizational units with established lines of communications.

3.3.1.2 INTEGRATE WBS AND OBS INTO THE RESPONSIBILITY ASSIGNMENT MATRIX (RAM)

Integrating the WBS on one axis of a matrix and the organizational structure on the other axis helps the team illustrate how the work and the responsible organization are integrated. Initially, the individual or team assigned the responsibility for any given element of work may or may not be identified. As with other aspects of the project, the OBS can evolve through the rolling wave process or in other phases of the project.

Following the initial work integration, the project manager collaborates with the appropriate organizational managers (frequently called functional or line managers) to identify the individual or team who will be assigned with the responsibility and authority for performing the work. That individual/team should participate, if not lead, the effort which determines and develops the budget and schedule to accomplish that work (i.e., the what, when, and how much of the work).

The responsibility assignment matrix (RAM) (see Figure 3-6 and the example in Appendix X4) shows the integration of the work in the WBS and the resource management structure in the OBS. In Figure 3-6, the OBS is structured with integrated project teams (IPTs), which group resources into teams. The RAM provides a visual that helps ensure each element of the project scope is assigned to a person or a team for management. The RAM delineates levels of control and responsibility and indicates the authority levels for the project.

The CAs for a project are determined by deciding which OBS and WBS intersections make up the CAs. All of the CAs do not need to be created at the same level of the WBS or OBS; therefore, many options are available to the project manager. Figure 3-6 noted two CAs which are at the same OBS level, but different WBS levels.

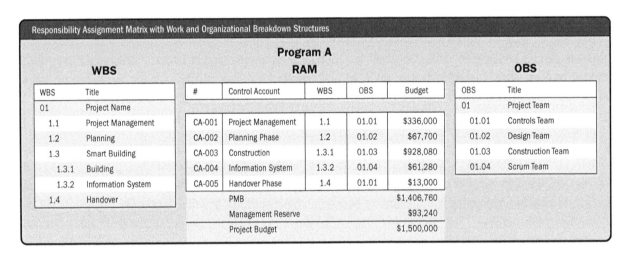

Figure 3-6. Example of Responsibility Assignment Matrix (RAM)

The CA is a management control point where scope, budget, actual cost, and schedule are integrated and compared to EV for performance measure. When determining whether a group of work (the WBS) and organizations (the OBS) should be pooled into a CA, the following considerations should be addressed:

◆ Will the work be performed by one or more functional organizations or a multifunctional integrated project team?

Using an integrated team may allow the effort to be collapsed into a single CA, while the use of various functional organizations may require a different CA for each responsible organization. Often, previous CAs close and new CAs open as the project migrates from one rolling wave milestone to another. The different CAs are created for the same WBS scope due to the changing nature of the team. One example of this is moving from a design focus team to a testing focus team.

◆ What level of the WBS is a logical point to manage? This can be influenced by:

- Make-or-buy decisions,
- Level of risk, and
- Level of criticality to the project, either cost, schedule, and/or performance.

◆ What is the availability of trained/capable CA managers?

◆ Will the work be divided up by project life cycle, control points, or reviews?

This is often done because the composition of a team usually changes when a WBS item passes through the project life cycle from design, first article, testing, or other phases.

When building the CA structure, it is important to include 100% of the WBS being measured across the project life cycle. That is, all of the work to be measured should be represented when the work within the CA is summarized. It is permissible for multiple organizations (frequently called performing organizations) to work on the scope within a CA; however, management responsibility and accountability belong to only one organization (the responsible organization). For EVM, the OBS needs to represent the responsible organization's structure with the responsible people or the empowered integrated project team (IPT). In many cases, the IPT has multifunctional or multiorganizational representation, which allows for teams to be more product oriented. This can result in the OBS structure aligning with the WBS structure.

Whenever work and budget moves into, out of, or within the project, one or more CAs change. Any change should always be reflected on the responsibility assignment matrix and authorized through change control. This approach provides the project manager with a continuously updated picture of all of the work and budget that is associated with a project. When CAs have only a planning package within a future rolling wave planning process, it's possible that a particular organization might not be identified; however, the WBS components should be clear and cover all of the work to be measured with EV within the PMB. In these cases, the control account should be owned by the project manager until the work is further broken out and assigned to a particular individual or team.

3.3.2 RISK MANAGEMENT

In order to navigate uncertainty, the outputs of the risk management processes as described in the *PMBOK®️ Guide* should be incorporated into the PMB. The objective of risk management is to exploit or enhance positive risks (opportunities) and to avoid or mitigate negative risks (threats) in order to optimize the chances of project success.

Risk management planning processes identify risks (see Section 11.2 of the *PMBOK® Guide*), analyze risks both qualitatively (Section 11.3 of the *PMBOK® Guide*) and quantitatively (Section 11.4 of the *PMBOK® Guide*), and plan risk responses (Section 11.5 of the *PMBOK® Guide*) for the uncertainties, both positive and negative, on the project baseline.

To incorporate risk considerations within the baselines, the project team conducts qualitative and quantitative risk analysis (scope, schedule, and cost) along with developing and incorporating into the baselines the planned risk responses. Integrating the outputs of the risk management processes with EVM enables early insight into scope, schedule, and cost estimates by comprehending the expected probability of a threat or opportunity occurrence related to schedule and cost estimate impact.

The project management plan incorporates risk responses/mitigations in various forms according to the risk management plan and risk register. Some responses may require updating the project baselines (cost, schedule, and scope) up front, while others may require changing the plan baselines only after reaching specific emerging circumstances (or risk triggers). The contingent responses should be planned and then included in work packages or planning packages. For example, a contingency plan may be implemented when the probability of a high-impact risk increases significantly after a risk trigger point has been reached, thus causing a replan of the baseline by moving the contingency to a specific WP/activity. EVM and risk management are best consolidated at the CA level under the responsibility of the manager of the CA. The movement of a contingency to a specific WP/activity goes through the change control process.

The implementation of risk responses, up front or later in the project, affects the expected rate at which the project work will be executed. The PMB should account for this factor. Information from the risk register, which may be included in the PMB, contains the items listed in Sections 3.3.2.1 and 3.3.2.2.

3.3.2.1 AGREED-UPON RESPONSE STRATEGIES

Risk responses, which usually involve effort for both negative and positive risks, impact the scope, schedule, and/ or cost baselines of specific CAs within the project. These responses need to be planned within the baseline work. Additionally, project resilience depends, in part, on how the project team sets the risk tolerance and risk appetite (risk avoidance or risk seeking) and to what extent contingency and/or management reserves are used. Stakeholder risk appetite should be considered and EVM variance thresholds appropriately adjusted depending on the established risk tolerance. Risk responses that are planned are incorporated into the PMB along with contingencies, while the management reserves are outside the baseline. The CA manager can handle the assigned risk and the responsibilities for managing the risk responses and contingencies on the project. Thus, the CA manager, in many instances, becomes the risk owner.

3.3.2.2 MANAGEMENT AND CONTINGENCY RESERVES

Contingency reserves are used for identified risks that are accepted and those risks for which contingent responses are devised. These reserves can fund contingency plans when they need to be implemented or can fund a necessary reaction to a risk after it occurs. Contingency reserves may be global to the overall project or may be allocated to specific control accounts.

Contingency reserves are not used for the purpose of masking overruns. Instead, these reserves are determined as a result of understanding identified risks and their potential impacts and are placed at the appropriate levels within the PMB. While it is expected that contingency reserves will be consumed to accommodate evolving risk responses or realized risk impact, there may be situations when the risk is either greater or lesser than initially estimated. In these cases, it is appropriate that a variance be recorded. Based on existing OPAs, the project team may decide, especially when impacts are significant, to adjust the future baseline through the change control process. The PMB is not going to be as effective as a management tool when the baseline is significantly different from the plan the project team is following. When reserves, whether too robust or not robust enough, have the team significantly off the baseline, the project team and stakeholders should consider baseline changes. Often, OPAs and EEFs drive environments when the original baselines are maintained for historical purposes while additional baselines are established for effective management of the remaining work.

The *PMBOK® Guide, The Standard for Risk Management in Portfolios, Programs, and Projects* [6], *Practice Standard for Project Risk Management* [7], *Practice Standard for Scheduling* [8], and *Practice Standard for Project Estimating* [9] cover additional information regarding the use of risk responses and reserves to address the impact of risks on the cost, schedule, or scope baselines. When using EV, any risk response, which includes activities that expend budget, needs to be assigned within a CA, and the activity captured in the project's scope, schedule, and cost baselines.

3.3.3 SCOPE BASELINE

The scope baseline, comprised of the project scope statement, WBS, and WBS dictionary, aligns with work and planning packages and provides information on all of the product and project deliverables against which execution and delivery are compared. Scope realization data, generated from the accomplishment of project scope, should be planned at the appropriate WBS activity level for WPs within the CAs. The basis for collecting the scope data is determined by the measurement method selected. The criteria, sometimes called the rules of credit, are outlined and documented during planning in the development of the project scope definition that is captured in the WBS dictionary and the WP and activities. Consideration should be given to deliverable quality.

When planning the scope baseline, the project team should consider how the scope data will be collected. The adequate measurement of the volume of scope accomplished based on a specific point in time and, especially at the end of each project control period (e.g., week, month), should be considered. The collection of scope realization and validation data includes information about project progress such as which activities or work packages have started, what their progress is, which have finished, and projecting when others will be accomplished. How this data is planned will impact how it is collected. It is used in the determination and measurement of EV and other EVM metrics as outlined in Section 4.4.

3.3.4 SCHEDULE BASELINE

The schedule baseline represents the approved version of a schedule model that can be changed using formal change control procedures and is used as the basis for comparison to actual results over time. When integrated with the project budget, the schedule baseline forms the basis for the development of the PMB. At any given point in time, and especially at the end of each project control period (e.g., week, month), the schedule data describe what and how much project work was planned to be performed.

The term *schedule* is often used to mean both the schedule model and the output of activities with associated dates. For clarity and consistency with the *PMBOK® Guide*, this standard defines (a) the project-specific data within the scheduling tool as *schedule model* and (b) the resulting outputs, based on the project-specific data, as *schedule model presentations*.

The schedule model includes all the time-related attributes used in the representation of the project management plan for executing the project's activities, for example, baseline start and finish dates, durations, dependencies, and other activity definitions and scheduling information. The basis for schedule data is outlined and documented during planning in the development of the integrated master schedule and determination of measurement methods to be used in the EVMS, as described in Section 3.2.2.2.

Developing the schedule model is the process of translating all of the WBS components into a sequential, time-phased model for project execution. Resource loading the schedule model at the activity level is not required for the application of EVM; however, it is a recommended practice that lends credibility to the PMB.

The project schedule integrates the activities associated with each WBS component and identifies dependencies between project activities as well as the dependencies that are external to the project. The schedule model can be decomposed and presented at various levels of detail.

This standard focuses on those schedule components having specific relevance to the practice of EVM. Therefore, for purposes of this section, it is assumed that the scheduling processes covered in the *PMBOK® Guide* are followed. For an overview of what is considered good practice on most projects most of the time for scheduling, refer to Section 6 of the *PMBOK® Guide*. For a more extensive treatment on the definition and implementation for project scheduling practices, refer to the *Practice Standard for Scheduling*.

3.3.4.1 SCHEDULE STRUCTURE

The schedule model, following good schedule practices, also needs to consider the need for EVM. The key is to build the schedule structure logic to not only reflect the WBS, but also the CA structure. Consider the integrated master schedule as the integration of all the individual CA detailed-level schedules. Within each CA's schedule, there should be a clear linkage to WPs and planning packages.

3.3.4.2 SCHEDULE AND BUDGET RELATIONSHIP

The relationship between the schedule model and the budgeting system is maintained throughout the life of the project. The PV is derived using the same assumptions as the scheduling model. The same WBS and set of other budget elements (CAs, WPs, and planning packages) should exist in both systems. Certain attributes of these, such as start and finish dates, budgets or weighting, and organizational responsibility, should always remain consistent between the budget and the schedule. The estimated cost (labor hours, direct material dollars or monetary units, travel, etc.) should be allocated to the work package or activity in the schedule that it supports, but it is not necessary. The minimum requirement is to allocate cost to the control account level. To ease the administrative burdens of keeping the cost and schedule baselines in sync, a resource-loaded (cost) schedule may be used. The result of the resource-loaded schedule is an integrated model of the time-phased budgeted plan. These schedules can also have the WBS dictionary, rules of credit based on the selected measuring method, basis of estimate for costs, and other information incorporated, thus providing a single model that represents the PMB.

Once the project schedule model is reviewed and agreed to by all of the project stakeholders, it is saved and stored as the project schedule baseline and forms the basis for the time-phased PMB. Section 4.6 addresses maintenance of the baselines.

3.3.4.3 SCHEDULE MODEL

The schedule model represents the time phasing for execution of the project's scope of work. The project schedule reflects the total project scope of work as defined in the WBS and, to a sufficient level of granularity, the plan, implementation, and control of the project. Both the high-level master schedule and the highest level of the WBS represent the overall project scope. Lower levels of the WBS correspond to equivalent levels of the schedule, extending this concept to control accounts, work packages, and planning packages. Figure 3-7 is the initial detailed schedule portion of the overall project schedule presentation. It represents the schedule model for the example in Appendix X4, which has activities over five quarters. Near-term activities are detail planned into work packages. The schedule is further detail planned during rolling waves (see the example in Appendix X4). Refer to the *Practice Standard for Scheduling* for further details on developing a schedule model.

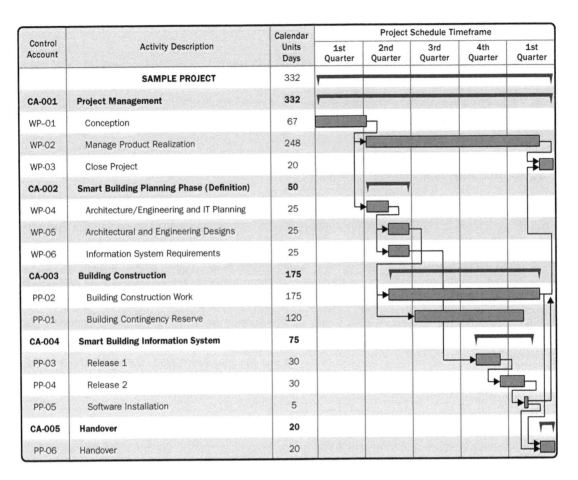

Control Account	Activity Description	Calendar Units Days	Project Schedule Timeframe				
			1st Quarter	2nd Quarter	3rd Quarter	4th Quarter	1st Quarter
	SAMPLE PROJECT	332					
CA-001	**Project Management**	**332**					
WP–01	Conception	67					
WP-02	Manage Product Realization	248					
WP-03	Close Project	20					
CA-002	**Smart Building Planning Phase (Definition)**	**50**					
WP-04	Architecture/Engineering and IT Planning	25					
WP-05	Architectural and Engineering Designs	25					
WP-06	Information System Requirements	25					
CA-003	**Building Construction**	**175**					
PP-02	Building Construction Work	175					
PP-01	Building Contingency Reserve	120					
CA-004	**Smart Building Information System**	**75**					
PP-03	Release 1	30					
PP-04	Release 2	30					
PP-05	Software Installation	5					
CA-005	**Handover**	**20**					
PP-06	Handover	20					

Figure 3-7. Project Schedule Presentation—Example

3.3.4.4 SCHEDULE EVOLUTION

Project budgeting and scheduling are iterative processes involving the negotiation of project constraints until consensus estimates are achieved among the stakeholders. Therefore, the schedule continues to evolve until the project manager establishes the PMB.

A properly structured schedule model depicts the project team's plan for work accomplishment by CA with WPs. The planning package should be planned in detail and broken down into WPs before the work is executed. The CA work package provides the underlying logic for the PMB, against which accomplishments are measured and expected future outcomes are forecasted.

Enhancements to the schedule model may include:

◆ Logic-driven schedule, networked at the work package or activity level,

◆ Resource-loaded WP and/or activities,

◆ Risk trigger milestones and potential risk responses incorporated as alternative paths, and

◆ Schedule risk analysis data incorporated into the schedule model.

Inclusion of probabilistic considerations based on complexity awareness and risk analysis (striking a balance between various risks and objectives) enhances the usefulness of the schedule model as a management tool.

3.3.5 COST BASELINE

The cost baseline for EVM is the approved budget for each control account with work and planning packages and the appropriate contingency reserve (when required, depending on EEFs/OPAs). For EVM, the cost for each work package or planning package (i.e., the approved budget) needs to be time-phased and aligned with the schedule baseline.

The cost baseline is developed as a summation of the approved budgets for the different CAs that have scheduled work or planning packages. The basis for cost data within each CA is outlined during planning for each CA. The cost should be based on cost estimates. The cost estimates are often broken out between direct and indirect costs. Whether indirect costs are in the project estimate and, therefore, in the project budget depends on EEFs and OPAs. EVM does not require any specific handling of indirect costs; however, indirect cost variances could impact variance analysis. When the project and the enterprise want to include indirect costs, these should be incorporated in the cost estimating process and included at the activity level or at higher levels (see Section 7.2.3.1 of the *PMBOK® Guide*). Within EVM, when allocated at high levels, indirect costs can be apportioned to control accounts, work packages, activities, or resources, as appropriate. It is important for users of EVM to understand which costs are included within the PMB and which are not; this is dependent on organizational rules. EVM requires the cost estimate to be aligned with the CAs at a minimum, but the cost estimate can be aligned down to the activity level.

The cost estimate provides the basis for establishing the budget. Typically, estimates should be developed for each work package or planning package. The estimates for each work package should be robust enough to assist the project team in planning the needed resources, while budget estimates for planning packages may have a lower level of detail until enough information is available to support the conversion to work packages. All cost estimates within the CAs should be developed within the timeframes established for that work in the schedule baseline. Further guidance for developing a cost estimate can be found in the *Practice Standard for Project Estimating* [9].

Once the cost estimates for work packages and planning packages within a control account are completed, the project manager and the control account manager review them. The project manager may decide to authorize budget for an amount more, less, or equal to the cost estimate as follows:

◆ More budget may be authorized if the project manager is aware of likely future events, such as changes in rates, processes, or customers. This extra budget is often put into contingency reserves at the work/planning package level or within the CA.

◆ Less budget may be authorized if the project manager is giving the control account manager a stretch goal or holding back reserve. Less budget may also be authorized if some of the assumptions in initial estimates are proven wrong or more information on scope is available before execution than when it was estimated. Often the budget below the cost estimate is placed in reserves outside the CA.

◆ Budget equal to the cost estimate may be authorized, particularly when risk analysis and reserves are handled outside of the control account.

The most universal and broad measurement unit used to value both budget and actual resource consumption is the monetary unit or appropriate currency, which is also the most widely used and original measure within the EVM method. On multicurrency projects, the management of exchange rates should be addressed, which can be done similarly to labor rate or other indirect and direct cost changes that have impacts on projects. This is not surprising since cost data answer the basic question of any project sponsor: How much is the project really costing the organization?

However, it is possible to use other units for budget and cost, such as labor hours (i.e., human effort). These alternatives often focus on a specific resource or cost element of the overall organizational effort, which is considered more relevant for management purposes. All other cost elements are either converted to this unit or simply not considered in EVM. The measure used depends on the nature and scope of the EVM being implemented and should be documented within the project management plan.

Alternative measures should be consistent with the boundaries of the cost elements being controlled by the project. For example, in some environments (e.g., in small software projects), the project manager is not responsible for measuring the full project cost but only the direct human effort. In these scenarios, labor hours are used as the measure of value—a more defined and less granular substitute for monetary units. In this example, nonhuman effort costs, such as travel costs, are outside of the PMB. As a result, the different costs of the hourly efforts are not captured within the PMB. In some cases, this may simplify the EVMS significantly while having little impact on the management value.

When alternative substitutes for monetary value are used, it is essential to ensure that the cost data used are the chosen measure of organizational effort (in the form of resource consumption) incurred to execute the project; such a measure, even if similar, should not be mistaken with the measures of scope accomplishment (e.g., scope data) like physical measures (e.g. drawings complete).

3.4 SETTING THE PERFORMANCE MEASUREMENT BASELINE (PMB)

The project team analyzes, consolidates, and integrates the information from the scope, schedule, and cost baselines. The baseline information incorporates the information from the risk registers and risk response plans.

The granularity of the PMB can be progressively elaborated throughout project planning and execution in an iterative process as the project scope, schedule, and cost estimates are refined into greater detail. Either tabular or graphical means can be used to display the information, but good practice suggests that both forms be developed. Although the PMB could be set manually, it is good practice to use software applications such as spreadsheets, scheduling software, or applications tailored for the implementation of EVM. At this point in the planning, for each baseline planned, the PMB can be set. The following have been accomplished and should now be recorded, reviewed, and validated into the PMB:

◆ Each work and planning package was estimated; therefore, each control account has a budget. The budget and the associated resources the budget represents is the total PV (i.e., the budget at completion [BAC]) for these scope components.

◆ Risk responses were developed, and each risk response cost was incorporated into work or planning package budgets or as contingency reserve, as appropriate.

◆ Undistributed budget was recorded for work authorized by the project charter and scope documentation, but has not yet been assigned to the control account level of the WBS.

◆ Each work and planning package was scheduled. They have planned dates when they should occur.

◆ Each CA was assigned to a responsible person or team.

◆ Methods of measurement were established to enable the reporting of the amount of scope or work accomplished once work enters a phase of execution.

◆ Methods were established to gather actual cost information associated with each CA at regular intervals, for example, every week or month.

At this point, the project has a combined scope, schedule, and cost into a time-phased, integrated baseline that represents costs over time (see Figure 3-8 and the example in Appendix X4). The PMB captures the scope's PV, which is time phased and establishes how actual work progress will be measured. Progress data and actual costs at the CA level are recorded into the PMB once the work begins. Using the PMB, EVM analyzes the actual performance in contrast to the baseline. Additionally, EVM uses the actual performance as a predictor for future performance.

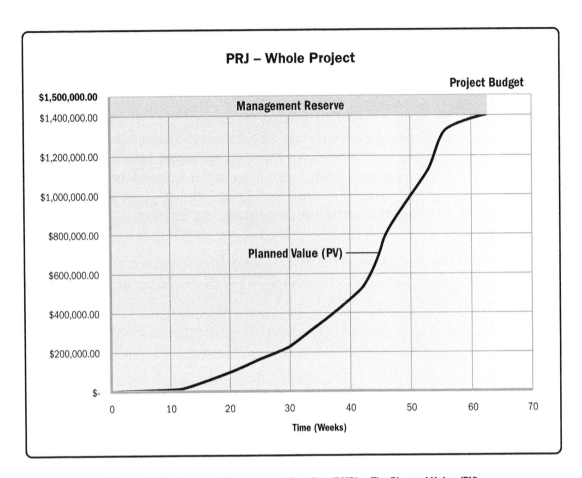

Figure 3-8. Performance Measurement Baseline (PMB)—The Planned Value (PV)

3.4.1 PROJECT BUDGET

The project budget is the sum of work and planning package cost estimates, the contingency reserve(s), and the management reserve. For EVM, the PMB part of the project budget includes the sum of the work and planning packages and contingency reserves within all of the CAs for which EVM will be performed. The project budget and PMB can be set in various ways, which depend on the OPAs and EEFs for the particular project or organization.

3.4.1.1 MANAGEMENT RESERVE (MR)

Management reserve is the time or budget that management sets aside in addition to the schedule or cost baseline. Management releases the management reserve for unforeseen work that is within the scope of the project. In most projects, and certainly in major projects, there is considerable uncertainty regarding the magnitude of future events or difficulties. To accommodate this uncertainty, a certain amount of the project budget can be identified as management reserve. The control of the management reserve depends on the OPAs and EEFs that the project team is working with.

The management reserve and the budget for the PMB are components of the project budget. The management reserve is typically not time phased and is not part of the PMB. As with contingency reserve, management reserve should not be used to mask performance-related overrun conditions. Rather, the contingency reserve is intended to be a budget for risk responses within the project charter's statement of work. The management reserve is for unforeseen risks that have had no anticipated risk responses established in the project management plan.

3.4.1.2 UNDISTRIBUTED BUDGET (UB)

Undistributed budget refers to project work within the PMB that has not yet been incorporated into a planned CA and, therefore, is typically not yet time phased. It is a temporary holding account for work and budget. OPAs should stipulate how UB is handled within the PMB, such as time phases at the end of the project.

3.4.1.3 CONTROL ACCOUNT (CA) BUDGETS

The next level below the project that provides a management control point is a CA. All work to be accomplished using EVM needs to be in a CA and further broken down into WPs. The accumulation of CA budgets should add up to the PMB with the addition of an undistributed budget. CA managers identify risks at their level. This may create some additional or alternative activities within certain WPs that may have uncertainties related to duration and/or cost. CA managers assign and time phase budgets for CAs and their corresponding work in accordance with an approved schedule, which may include both direct and indirect costs. CAs are time phased according to the rolling wave concept, which requires detailed planning of work packages for a specified number of EV reporting time periods before the scheduled start of the work. The budget at completion (BAC) for each CA is the sum of the work packages, planning packages, and contingency reserve budgets.

3.4.2 ESTABLISHING THE PMB

The PMB consists of three baselines integrated into one. Typically, as part of setting the baseline, there is a process (either documented in an OPA or called for in an EEF) where the work described under the baseline is authorized, tracked, and funded. Additionally, as each CA is a segregated part of the project that is managed, the project team frequently develops and maintains a CA plan that captures the specifics of the CA.

3.4.2.1 AUTHORIZE THE WORK

Authorization is the formal permission and direction to begin a specific project effort, which, typically, is a CA. It is a method for sanctioning project work to ensure that the work is done by the identified organization, at the right time, in the proper sequence, and within the approved baseline. In its simplest form, the work authorization process follows these steps:

◆ **Step 1.** The project manager receives authorization to proceed with the project by means of a project charter or customer contract/authorization. This authorization may include limits on the funds available to the project manager, which is the amount of budget that is authorized.

◆ **Step 2.** The project manager authorizes the next tier of management to proceed with the assigned work, usually by issuing a work authorization document. Typically, this next level is the CA level, but there could be one or more additional levels between the total project and the CAs. If so, each level receives its own authorization and then continues the authorization within its prescribed, unbroken chain of authorization.

◆ **Step 3.** In some organizations, functional manager concurrence or authorization may be required.

◆ **Step 4.** The CA manager may authorize specific individuals to begin work and provide the scope, planned budget (often in hours), and charge numbers required to be used.

3.4.2.2 PROJECT BUDGET LOG

The project budget log is the central repository for all project budgets. At any time, the project manager should be able to review the project budget log and obtain a complete accounting of the value and classification for every element of the project budget in addition to changes to the budget throughout the life of the project. As work is authorized for control accounts, entries are made in the project budget log to show the movement of budget from the undistributed budget to the distributed budget. When the entire project is authorized into control accounts (or control accounts and summary-level budgets), the value of the undistributed budget will be zero. Within CAs, the budget is authorized to work or planning packages. An example of the initial project budget log is shown in Figure 3-9. A broader example is shown in Appendix X4.

Budget Log				
Date	**From Account**	**To Account**	**Amount**	**Description**
6-January	Corporate	Project	$1,500,000	Program budget
6-January	Project	CA-001	$336,000	Initial fund CA
6-January	Project	CA-002	$67,700	Initial fund CA
6-January	Project	CA-003	$928,080	Initial fund CA
6-January	Project	CA-004	$61,280	Initial fund CA
6-January	Project	CA-005	$13,700	Initial fund CA
7-January	Project	MR	$93,240	Create MR account
8-January	CA-01	WP-01	$19,840	Authorize WP-01
8-January	CA-01	WP-02	$297,600	Authorize WP-02

Figure 3-9. Project Budget Log Example

3.4.2.3 PROJECT FUNDING REQUIREMENTS

Total funding requirements and periodic funding requirements are determined based on the project cost estimates and time-phased budget. When available funding is not consistent with the required funding, the project may need to be replanned to meet funding constraints. The project funding requirements are then updated to agree with the budgetary decisions made to establish the PMB.

3.4.2.4 CONTROL ACCOUNT PLAN

The detailed plan for a CA is called a CA plan. The CA plan contains all elements and aspects of the control account, some of which include:

◆ Name of the responsible CA manager;

◆ Description of the work scope to be done;

◆ Specific milestones to be accomplished;

◆ WPs that delineate the scope, schedule, and budget (incrementally, cumulative to date, and at completion) for specific, well-defined tasks within the CA;

◆ Planning packages that delineate the scope, schedule, and budget (incrementally, cumulative to date, and at completion) for specific future tasks within the control account; and

◆ Estimates to complete, which should be time phased and may lead to an up-to-date representation of the total expected funding needed (the estimate at completion [EAC]).

3.4.3 BUDGET VERSUS FUNDING

One of the key aspects of EVM is the specific terminology related to budget and funds. Budget is a work planning element that is earned (i.e., the EV) when the corresponding work is completed. Funds (i.e., remaining funds) are the amount of money that is available to accomplish the work. Often this is controlled by an organization's work authorization system, which allows the project manager to manage situations when full funding is not provided.

3.5 APPLYING EVM IN AN AGILE/HYBRID ENVIRONMENT

When using agile approaches, the need for an organization to achieve the benefit of managing sets of projects or CAs in a coordinated manner is the same as using a plan-driven approach. All project teams should ensure that work is aligned to key business objectives. It is important that management at all levels can see that the overall progress is measured, risks are managed, and the wider view across the project is maintained.

As mentioned in Table A1-2 of the *Agile Practice Guide* for the Project Schedule Management Knowledge Area, organizations are becoming aware that they do not need to adhere to a single methodology (e.g., predictive or various forms of agile). This knowledge has led to the creation of hybrid concepts. The project manager in an agile environment is responsible for managing and tracking the business, technical, and delivery aspects of the project throughout its life cycle. In addition, the project manager provides high-level management direction and coordination for planning, leading, organizing, and motivating the hybrid project teams. The agile project manager may also be responsible for managing several concurrent high-visibility projects or CAs using a mixture of plan-driven and agile approaches in a fast-paced environment that may cross multiple business divisions.

This standard considers agile in the same manner as outlined in the *Agile Practice Guide*. This standard is intended for project teams that find themselves in the messy middle ground between predictive and agile approaches (see *Agile Practice Guide*, p. 4). This section explains how to align a project team's agile, iterative, or other adaptive environment approach with the rest of the project using EV. The key to this approach is alignment of the project's CA structure with an agile approach. Within this section, the term *agile* is used to mean agile, iterative, or other adaptive approaches.

The PMB's structural component is a collection of CAs; therefore, the key for integrating agile-driven work is to define how the agile work fits into the project's CAs. It is important for the project team to determine how the agile efforts will be mapped into one or more CAs. For complex agile delivery initiatives, the CA scope may be broken down into smaller, more manageable autonomous units (e.g. epics, capabilities, and/or features) of the solution with the schedule of each CA decomposed into work and planning packages containing the actual activities (e.g., features and/or user stories) needed to deliver the solution. For purposes of the process illustration in Figure 3-10, Control Account CA-002's scope corresponds to the solution to be delivered by the solution integration agile team with WPs (i.e., the point where work is planned, progress is measured, and EV is assessed) defined as Release-1 and Release-2. Figure 3-10 shows four CAs of a project combining plan-driven approaches with an adaptive approach (i.e., a hybrid approach). At the end of each reporting period (e.g., week #48), progress is compared to the PMB for each CA and the resulting EV data is rolled up to the overall project's EVM reporting status.

Projects can use Scrum framework measures as inputs to EVM calculations. As stated in Section 5.4.1 of the *Agile Practice Guide*, agile approaches do not define how to manage and track costs to evaluate expected return on investment information. (For more information on other agile practices, see Section 5 of the *Agile Practice Guide*.) EVM's cost performance index (CPI) provides a measure of efficiency regarding the resources consumed relative to the work accomplished. Also, the to-complete cost performance index (TCPI) forecasts desired efficiency to ensure the work is completed on budget. Additionally, traditional agile metrics (as defined in Section 5.4 of the *Agile Practice Guide*) do not provide estimates of cost at completion for the release, nor do they supply cost metrics to support the business when they consider making decisions like changing requirements in a release as would be rationalized by an EVMS analysis for traditional projects. However, for managing and reporting on hybrid projects with agile and EVM components at regular reporting intervals, the project manager should convert the data points from the agile component into the required EVM unit of measure for analyzing the overall PMB and for consolidated EVMS reporting. For more details on reporting for hybrid projects, see Section 4.5.1.1 of this standard.

Smart Building Example		Performance Schedule		
	Work Packages/Sprints	Start	End	
CA-002 (Building Planning)	**Smart Building Planning Phase**			
	Architectural/Engineering and IT Planning	6-Apr	8-May	
	Architectural/Engineering Designs	11-May	12-Jun	
CA-003 (Building Construction)	**Conversion to Smart Building**			
	Mobilization and Site Clearing	15-Jun	24-Jul	
	Civil Works	27-Jul	8-Jan	
	Electrical System	19-Oct	8-Jan	
	Mechanical Equipment	2-Nov	25-Dec	
	IT Infrastructure	2-Nov	13-Nov	
	External Area	11-Jan	22-Jan	
	Commissioning	25-Jan	29-Jan	
CA-004 (Smart Building Information System)	**Agile Delivery Solution Integration**			
	Release-1 (Work Package-1)			
	Sprint-01: Create Security/Notification/Alarm Systems	19-Oct	30-Oct	
	Sprint-02: Create Smart Building Dashboard/Scorecard Reports	2-Nov	13-Nov	
	Sprint-03: Create Climate Control System	16-Nov	27-Nov	
	Release-2 (Work Package-2)			
	Sprint-04: Create Smart Building Entertainment System	30-Nov	11-Dec	
	Sprint-05: Create Analytics and Augmented Intelligence System	14-Dec	25-Dec	
	Sprint-06: Integration and Performance Testing	28-Dec	8-Jan	
CA-005 (Handover)	**Smart Building Handover**			
	Acceptance Testing	1-Feb	19-Feb	
	Building User Testing	22-Feb	26-Feb	

Original period ending week #48 ➡️

⬅️ New period

Figure 3-10. Integrated Project Schedule

When integrating agile approaches within a PMB, a minimal set of input parameters are needed: the budget cost of the effort for each CA (the cost), an estimated product backlog (the scope), a release plan that provides information on the number of iterations in the release, and the assumed velocity (i.e., how much of the solution is the project team able to deliver per iteration). Estimates for scope can be in story points or whatever method the team is using to estimate the effort. It is critical, however, that a numerical estimate of the scope be established. For this section, story points are used as a measure of user story effort and velocity, as covered in Section 5.4.1 of the *Agile Practice Guide*.

In agile environments, the PMB equivalent is expressed as the scope of work planned for the release or *planned value* (PV). This allows for course corrections to be made without disruption to, or a rebaselining of, the PMB. The current release plan is compared against the actual work performed.

In summary, when using an agile approach within EVM, it is important to know the following for each control account:

◆ **Scope.** In agile approaches, the scope represents the total number of story points planned and how they are phased within iterations and/or releases.

◆ **Planned value (PV):**

 ▪ PV is the authorized budget assigned to scheduled work.

 ▪ In agile environments, PV is the sum of the estimated user story sizes across all iterations, budgeted for completion up until the planned date.

◆ **Earned value (EV):**

 ▪ EV is the measure of work performed.

 ▪ In agile environments, EV represents the value of work completed (i.e., measured by the total number of story points for all completed user stories multiplied by the number of completed iterations) and also expressed in terms of the budget authorized for that work (i.e., story points by labor costs). EV can be reported for cumulative to date or for a specific reporting period.

◆ **Estimate at completion (EAC):**

 ▪ EAC is the expected total cost of completing all work expressed as the sum of the actual cost to date and the estimate to complete (ETC).

 ▪ In an agile environment, EAC is the expected total cost of the agile effort calculated as actual cost (i.e., total number of completed story points × team's labor cost per story point) + estimate to complete (i.e., *average velocity* × planned number of remaining iterations × team's *labor cost per story point*).

◆ **Key assumption.** The key assumption in agile environments is that the ratio of story points completed to the total story points planned for a release is a good measure of the actual percent complete.

The project team needs to decide how to map iterations to the CA level or the WP level of the PMB structure. With the agile work mapped to an EV structure, EVM metrics can be used to measure the incremental progress the solution completed at the end of each iteration (i.e., cumulative velocity). See Section 4.5.1.1 for more details on converting the agile effort to be in sync with EVM reporting requirements. More details on the actual EVM calculations for the agile effort are included in Section 4 and Appendix X4.

Once all of the information is collected (i.e., scope, PV, EV, EAC, and key assumption), the project manager can set a baseline with each agile team within a CA or WP. One important thing to keep in mind when determining progress with agile teams is that at the end of the iteration a user story is either completed or not completed, and the team does not get partial credit for unfinished user stories. There is no percentage of completion or partial value for an incomplete user story.

Agile release planning provides a high-level summary timeline of the release schedule (typically 3 to 6 months) based on the product roadmap and the product vision for the product's evolution. Agile release planning also determines features to be developed along with the number of iterations or sprints in the release planning. It also allows the product owner and team to decide how much scope needs to be developed and how long it will take to have a releasable product based on business goals, dependencies, and impediments. For more details on planning in an agile environment, see Section 6.5.2.8 of the *PMBOK® Guide*.

Since features represent value to the customer, the timeline provides a more easily understood project schedule as it defines which features will be available at the end of each iteration, which is exactly the depth of information the customer is looking for. The approach is to map the agile team deliverable schedule to the timeline of the PMB structure. There is more than one way to do the mapping (see example in Figure 3-10).

4

EXECUTING, MONITORING, AND CONTROLLING

The Executing Process Group consists of those processes performed to complete the work defined in the project management plan to satisfy the project requirements.

The Monitoring and Controlling Process Group consists of those processes required to (a) track, review, and regulate the progress and performance of the project; (b) identify any areas in which changes to the plan are required; and (c) initiate the corresponding changes.

4.1 OVERVIEW

As outlined in Section 3, one benefit of using earned value management (EVM) is that it encourages, reinforces, and in some cases, requires that best practices for project planning are put into place. Therefore, it is believed that EVM enhances the project planning process. While applying the Executing and the Monitoring and Controlling processes, EVM brings about new concepts and elements that are unique to the use of EVM that would not be implemented otherwise. Figure 4-1 depicts the Project Management Process Groups and processes (with specific sections) from the *PMBOK® Guide* and their relevance to employing EVM on a project. It also outlines the general structure for this section.

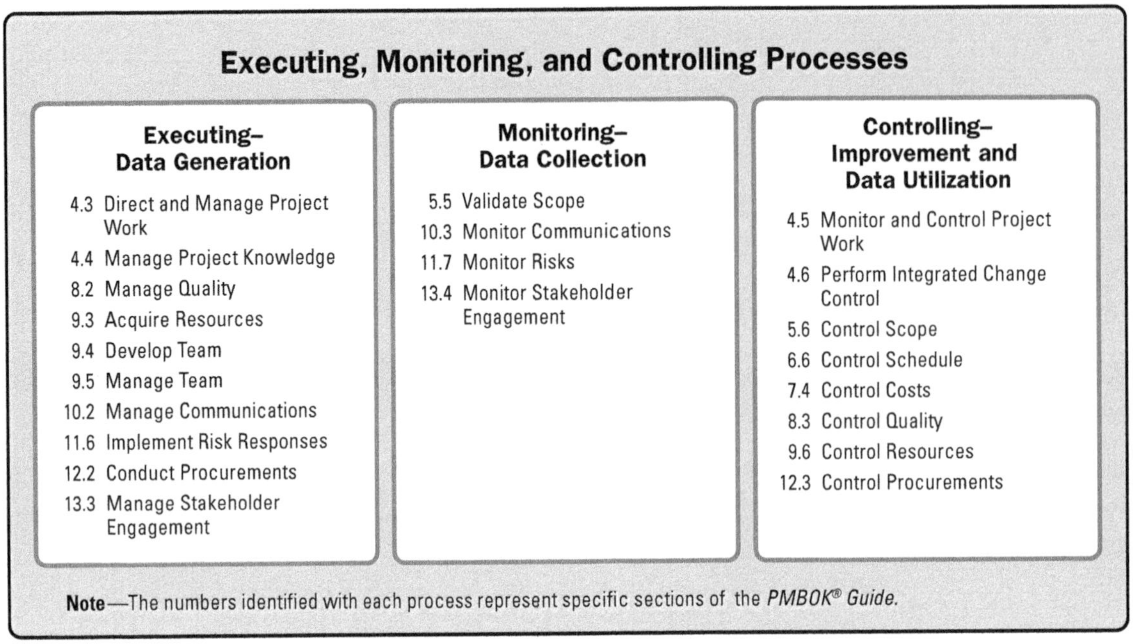

Executing, Monitoring, and Controlling Processes

Executing–
Data Generation

4.3 Direct and Manage Project Work

4.4 Manage Project Knowledge

8.2 Manage Quality

9.3 Acquire Resources

9.4 Develop Team

9.5 Manage Team

10.2 Manage Communications

11.6 Implement Risk Responses

12.2 Conduct Procurements

13.3 Manage Stakeholder Engagement

Monitoring–
Data Collection

5.5 Validate Scope

10.3 Monitor Communications

11.7 Monitor Risks

13.4 Monitor Stakeholder Engagement

Controlling–
Improvement and
Data Utilization

4.5 Monitor and Control Project Work

4.6 Perform Integrated Change Control

5.6 Control Scope

6.6 Control Schedule

7.4 Control Costs

8.3 Control Quality

9.6 Control Resources

12.3 Control Procurements

Note—The numbers identified with each process represent specific sections of the *PMBOK® Guide*.

Figure 4-1. Earned Value (EV): Executing, Monitoring, and Controlling Processes

While applying the Executing and the Monitoring and Controlling processes, the project team uses the EVM system (EVMS) to promptly obtain verified project performance information and metrics to create the most objective, accurate, and timely project performance reports by seeking to:

◆ Eliminate or reduce undesired variation.

◆ Exploit opportunities to improve project performance and its business value.

◆ Engage all stakeholders so that there is a common understanding about how the project is unfolding.

◆ Engage management and stakeholders in devising and supporting effective project management decisions.

During this project management phase, the EVMS is the primary basis for managing project performance, possibly in conjunction with other project analysis tools (e.g., critical path analysis). This includes (a) measuring, analyzing, and reporting performance; (b) taking corrective and preventive actions where needed; (c) managing project changes; and (d) maintaining the performance measurement baseline (PMB) to ensure traceability and its integrity.

Data collection processes should be in place to ensure both the timeliness and the consistency of the data that are used to produce performance metrics. The data include measures regarding (a) project scope and technical performance, (b) time and schedule, and (c) resource consumption and associated costs. The data are the basis for undertaking auditable and objective analyses of the project performance and its causes through the production of various performance metrics.

Performance analysis provides insight into the causes of observed past variations and future project trends. This is essential for engaging management and project stakeholders to consider the best planning options and support the required decisions to move the project toward improved performance. EVM-based performance management is also important for improving the effectiveness and quality of reporting and communications, stimulating an open and proactive project management culture, and increasing trust among the stakeholders.

An effective EVMS creates opportunities to maintain control over scope, cost, and schedule. When project changes are approved, the PMB is updated, then traceability and integrity are maintained. This is an essential aspect of an EVMS, because the baseline is the means to measure performance. This process should be both timely and rigorous, and it should ensure adequate communication to stakeholders.

In project management, the project team seeks the continuous improvement of the project management plan and supporting management processes. The EVMS follows this same principle. While applying executing, monitoring, and controlling processes, the use of EVMS provides information and experience that can be used as the basis for continuous improvement. This makes the EVMS more effective and efficient in helping the project team to gear the project toward success. The EVMS, as devised during planning, often requires adjustments throughout the executing processes. Examples of these adjustments include data collection procedures, training stakeholders, improving communications, revising roles and responsibilities, improving the information system, or changing the reporting formats to address emerging priorities.

4.2 EXECUTING

While applying the executing processes, data about the project's actual performance are generated. At this time, the project scope is accomplished and a large portion of the project budget, resources, and time are expended. The goal of executing in this standard is not to describe the processes outlined within the *PMBOK® Guide*, but instead to focus on the management activities that are required based on the decision to use EVM—implementing the EVM system and developing specific competency on EVM.

4.2.1 SYSTEM IMPLEMENTATION

As described in Section 2, an EVMS comprises working processes, stakeholders' roles and responsibilities, supporting IT infrastructure, and a process owner. While the work and effort required may vary, the implementation of the EVMS becomes part of the project scope as a deliverable; therefore, it is incorporated into the project management plan.

While Section 3 refers to the use of the EVMS in planning, Section 4 outlines the implementation and use of the EVMS. This process follows a timeline that is compatible with project management requirements.

Once the EVMS is implemented, information related to scope, schedule, and cost data become available for project performance analysis. This provides leadership with valid, timely forecasts and feedback to guide project management decision making toward project success.

The effective implementation and use of an EVMS for the overall benefit of the project requires stakeholders to have the required knowledge, skills, and abilities to interact with the system and make adequate use of the information it provides. These competencies should be verified and monitored, and when required, additional training should be considered.

4.2.2 COMPETENCY AND CAPABILITY DEVELOPMENT

Following the guidelines in Section 9.4 of the *PMBOK® Guide* for the Develop Team process, the project management plan, project documents, enterprise environmental factors (EEFs), and organizational process assets (OPAs) are reviewed to determine the need for developing and improving stakeholders' competencies regarding project management. In particular, these competencies are the knowledge, skills, and abilities required to ensure the EVMS is deployed and used effectively to address the project management needs of the environment.

4.2.2.1 PROFESSIONAL DEVELOPMENT

Professional development increasingly plays an important part in organizational success. Acquiring personal and team competencies for performance management improves productivity performance at the portfolio, program, and project levels. These competencies primarily include training on EVM and underlying disciplines such as scheduling, cost estimating, and risk management. For additional information on competencies, refer to *Project Manager Competency Development Framework (PMCDF)* [10]. Organizations should develop and implement a sustained, systematic effort to develop knowledge, experience, attitudes, abilities, and skills toward the successful application of an EVMS to attain effective performance management. Strong matrix and projectized organizations, in particular, usually incorporate training in performance management through their employee development program and focus on knowledge sharing. This training may be part of a learning organization initiative and focus on knowledge sharing. EVM training may focus on the short-term gains for the purpose of enhancing benefits in an expedient manner. Timeliness of training helps to achieve sustainable buy-in from senior management from an early stage of implementation.

The project manager and those responsible for managing the EVMS proactively interact with the various project stakeholders to create a positive influence for fulfilling the various needs of the project. They should seek ways to develop relationships that assist the team in achieving the goals and objectives of the project. In addition, they should maintain a strong advocacy role within the organization.

Depending on the organizational structure, the project team members responsible for the EVMS may report to a functional manager. In other cases, project managers may report to a PMO or a portfolio or program manager who is ultimately responsible for one or more enterprise-wide projects. In this case, project managers should work closely with the portfolio or program manager to achieve the project objectives and to ensure the project management plan aligns with the portfolio or program management plan.

4.2.2.2 PROFESSIONAL DISCIPLINE

Continuing knowledge transfer and integration is important for effectively managing the project and the EVMS. This knowledge and development are ongoing in the project management profession and in related areas (e.g., EVM), where the project team maintains subject matter expertise. This knowledge transfer and integration includes, but is not limited to:

◆ Contribution of knowledge and expertise to others within the profession at the local, national, and global levels (e.g., communities of practice, international organizations); and

◆ Participation in continuing education and development in the following:

■ Profession itself (e.g., universities and PMI),

■ Related professions (e.g., systems engineering and configuration management), and

■ Other professions (e.g., information technology and aerospace).

4.2.2.3 INDUSTRY TRENDS

The project team, and specifically those responsible for managing the EVMS, should be knowledgeable about current industry trends and continually evaluate to determine how new trends can impact or apply to current projects. These trends include but are not limited to:

◆ Agile approaches for small or large complex environments;

◆ Product development;

◆ Standards (e.g., project management, contract management, quality management, and agile approaches);

◆ Technical support tools;

◆ Economic forces that impact the immediate project;

◆ Influences affecting the project management discipline; and

◆ Sustainability strategies.

4.2.2.4 DEVELOPING COMPETENCIES AND CAPABILITIES

As mentioned in Section 4.2.2, the project management plan should include the required competency and capability development activities for a successful implementation of the EVMS. This includes proactively identifying the skills and knowledge of all stakeholders that may require enhancement or development regarding the use of EVM.

The main goal of these activities is to ensure that the adequate level of individual competencies and organizational capabilities exist to address the use of EVMS. For example, the use of EVM requires that cost estimating, scheduling, and risk management competencies exist at adequate levels of maturity, and that organizational resources and processes are in place to support mature practices in these areas.

During execution, it is important to ensure that these planned activities are implemented in a timely manner. It is also important to monitor the effectiveness of the activities and identify, plan, and execute additional activities, as needed.

4.3 COLLECTING DATA

In order to measure and analyze project performance, data are first collected for each of the project's key performance dimensions: scope, schedule, and cost. The cost management plan, schedule management plan, scope management plan, and any other subsidiary management plans that form the project management plan (see Section 4.2.3.1 of the

PMBOK® Guide) provide guidance for the data collection process, performance measurement methods, periods, and units required to populate the EVMS.

The EVM data collection and analysis process is devised in planning and continuously improved during the executing, monitoring, and controlling processes. Collecting data should be commensurate with the project's size, complexity, and importance to the organization to ensure the EVMS is effective, efficient, and adding value to the overall project management process.

Making use of the already existing data collection processes in the organization (OPAs) is considered a best practice. This should be pursued during planning to promote data quality and efficiency of the EVMS, with the required resources being identified and available during execution.

4.3.1 SCOPE DATA

Data generated from the accomplishment of the scope during execution (scope realization data) are collected into work packages within the control accounts (CAs). Scope data are collected, as necessary, to ensure the adequate measurement of the volume of scope accomplished based on a specific point in time, and especially at the end of each project control period (e.g., week, month). The collection of scope realization data includes information about project progress, including which deliverables or work packages have started, what their progress is, upcoming activities, and which have finished. Once this information is collected, it is used in the determination and measurement of EV and other EVM metrics, as outlined in Section 4.4.

The scope data to be collected depend primarily on the measurement method established during planning (see Section 3.2.2.2) for the deliverable or work package, for example:

◆ **Physical scope units.** Examples include meters (m), square meters (m^2), cubic meters (m^3), number of pages, number of drawings, feet of pipe installed, yards of concrete poured, story points, function points.

◆ **Milestones or events.** Examples include started, draft submitted, under review, approved.

◆ **Effort consumed by a type of resource.** Examples include person hours, person months.

◆ **Time elapsed.** Examples include days, weeks, and months (e.g., supervision).

To illustrate this further, see Appendix X4.

4.3.2 SCHEDULE DATA

The schedule baseline represents the time-phased execution of the project's scope of work. At a specific point in time, and especially at the end of each project control cycle, schedule data are collected to help identify and measure the scope accomplished, and is used in estimating expected durations, start dates, and completion dates. As a minimum, schedule data include the following data regarding the project for updating the schedule:

◆ Actual start date of initiated activities,

◆ Actual finish date of completed activities,

◆ Updated estimate for start date of uninitiated activities,

◆ Updated estimate for finish date of uncompleted activities, and

◆ Updated estimate for dependencies (logic) and associated leads and lags.

While the schedule baseline is not changed at this point, the proposed schedule updates about the project's future should reflect the best estimates produced by the project team, in particular from those with the role of control account (CA) managers, given the current project status.

4.3.3 COST DATA

Monitoring and controlling entails collecting cost data to determine the actual value of the resource consumption incurred based on a specific point in time and especially at the end of every project control status cycle (e.g., week, month). The actual value of resource consumption is a measure of the overall organizational effort already incurred to accomplish the project scope. Cost data collected are also used in estimating the expected resource consumption for the project scope remaining to be accomplished. The collection of cost data should be consistent with the basis for cost data established in the PMB.

As described in Section 3.2.3, the most universal and broad measurement unit used to value both budget and actual resource consumption is the monetary unit (dollars, euros, pounds, or other currency). It is also possible to use other units for budget and cost, such as labor hours (i.e., human effort). These alternatives often focus on a specific resource or cost element from the overall organizational effort that is considered more relevant for management purposes. When these alternative substitutes for monetary value are used, it is essential to ensure that the cost data used are the chosen measure for the organizational effort (in the form of resource consumption) to execute the project. This measure should not be confused with the measures of scope accomplishment (i.e., scope data), for example, physical measures (e.g., m², drawings).

To summarize, the collection of cost data includes the information on efforts that have been authorized and incurred and may include both direct and indirect costs. Cost data provide a measure of what has been invested, whereas scope data are a measure of what has been delivered. This information, once collected, processed, and organized, is used to determine the actual cost to date.

4.4 MANAGING PERFORMANCE

Managing performance is the process of comparing actual cost, schedule, and scope accomplishment to the PMB for the purposes of analyzing and diagnosing the status of the CAs and overall project and, whenever adequate, making decisions to improve project performance. Performance analysis provides for early indications or trends for the expected final costs and schedule completion as well as understanding the risk environment. This analysis supports predictions and trends for future project performance and outcomes, and informs about required changes to the baseline.

By deploying an EVMS on the project, various metrics can be produced that address the project's cost, schedule, and scope for past, current, and future conditions. These metrics, represented in many data forms and/or graphics, provide an effective means to communicate a common understanding of the project to all stakeholders.

Managing performance requires that a number of inputs are available in the EVMS in a timely and synchronized manner. The following components in the project management plan are used to analyze project performance:

◆ **Performance measurement baseline (PMB).** The PMB is used to compare planned performance with actual performance to determine project status.

◆ **Variance thresholds**. These thresholds establish the acceptable range of variance according to the tolerances of the project team, management, sponsors, and other stakeholders. These thresholds are the basis to implement management by exception (e.g., once these thresholds are exceeded, the project sponsor and/or governance may be called upon to intervene).

◆ **Subsidiary management plans.** The cost management plan, schedule management plan, scope management plan, risk management plan, and any other management plans that are used to provide guidance in managing and controlling the project.

Performance analysis relies on work performance information generated from data collected about project progress, specifically regarding its three dimensions of performance: scope, schedule, and cost data, as previously described in Section 4.3.

EVM performance analysis relies on the following data points for a given moment in time:

◆ **Planned value (PV).** The authorized budget assigned to scheduled work. At a point in time, it is the total budget allocated to the amount of work that was planned to be performed.

◆ **Earned value (EV).** The measure of work performed expressed in terms of the budget authorized for that work. At a point in time, it is the total budget allocated to the amount of work that was performed.

◆ **Actual cost (AC).** The realized cost incurred for the work performed. At a point in time, it is the total cost incurred with the resources consumed for the work performed.

◆ **Earned schedule (ES).** The time allocated in the baseline to complete the cumulative amount of work that was performed at a point in time.

◆ **Actual time (AT).** The time that actually elapsed to complete the cumulative amount of work that was performed at a point in time.

◆ **Budget at completion (BAC).** The sum of all budgets established for the work to be performed. It is the approved budget to complete the entire work scope.

◆ **Schedule at completion (SAC).** The total schedule duration established to complete the entire work scope.

The planned value (PV) is represented in the performance measurement baseline (PMB), as is the budget at completion (BAC). The earned value (EV) and actual cost (AC) are updated from data collected as the project progresses. EV can be determined by various methods. The EVM considered to plan the baseline should be used consistently to determine EV during execution. Earned schedule (ES) is derived mathematically from EV and the PMB. Actual time (AT) is the time at which the EV accrued is recorded.

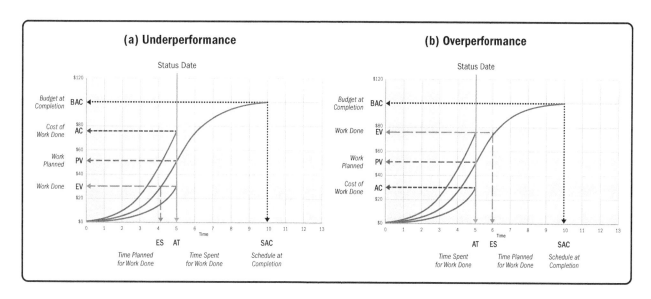

Figure 4-2. Graphical View of the EVM Performance Data Points

Figure 4-2 provides a graphical representation of EVM data points showing both underperformance and overperformance scenarios. As it can be observed, the amount for work that is accomplished in a project can be more or less than the amount of work planned in the PMB.

When EV is less than PV, this indicates that the total amount of work that is behind schedule in the project (negative variance) is greater than the total amount of work that is ahead of schedule (positive variance). Conversely, when EV is greater than PV, this indicates that the total amount of work ahead of schedule in the project (positive variance) is greater than the total work that is behind schedule (negative variance). It is important to note that an overall positive variance does not necessarily mean that the work is being executed according to the sequence planned in the schedule baseline.

For the current amount of work performed in the project (EV), a certain amount of time should have elapsed according to the baseline. Earned schedule (ES) is this time at which the current amount of EV accrued should have been earned. For example, if ES = 4 months, this means that the total amount of work accomplished to date should have been performed by month 4. As it can be observed in Figure 4-2, when the ES (time that should have elapsed given the amount of work accomplished) is compared against AT (time that actually elapsed), a difference indicates that either more or less time has been spent than planned with the amount of work performed. As with EV and PV, it is important to note that when ES is equal to or greater than AT (positive variance), it does not necessarily mean that the work is being performed according to the planned sequence in the schedule baseline.

When AC is compared with EV, a variance shows either cost savings or cost overruns. Both AC and EV refer to the same scope, where AC is the actual cost incurred and EV is the cost budgeted for that same scope. As shown in Figure 4-2, the actual cost of the work accomplished can be more or less than the budget planned in the baseline for that same work. When AC is equal to or less than EV (positive variance), the aggregate cost savings are greater than the possible cost overruns. Conversely, when AC is greater than EV (negative variance), the aggregate cost overruns are greater than the possible cost savings.

4.4.1 VARIANCE RESPONSE

EVM performance analysis includes the calculation of several variance measures that help to determine and understand the status of a project. The benefit of EVM is to provide information early so that variation can be managed effectively through management intervention. It may also help to indicate when the risk management process is ineffective and requires improvement.

A variance is a quantifiable deviation or departure from a known baseline or expected value. Variance analysis in EVM is the explanation, including cause, impact, and corrective and improvement actions (when appropriate) for scope, schedule, and cost variation from the PMB.

4.4.1.1 COST VARIANCE

Cost variance (CV) measures the difference between the budget approved in the baseline to be spent for the work accomplished and the realized cost incurred with the resources consumed to accomplish that same work. It answers the following management questions related to cost performance:

◆ Are we spending more or less than budgeted for the work done?

◆ How much more or less are we spending?

Both budget and incurred cost are measured by the unit of measure selected for the EVMS (see Section 4.3). This is a measure of CV; it measures either the overrun or the savings with the work accomplished.

As of the date of examination, the equation used to express CV is:

$$CV = EV - AC$$

When the variance is equal to 0, it means that as much budget as planned has been spent for the work accomplished. When CV is negative, the work accomplished is costing more than planned. When CV is positive, the work is costing less than planned. CV can also be expressed in percent relative to EV:

$$CV_w\% = CV/EV$$

Figure 4-3 illustrates CV.

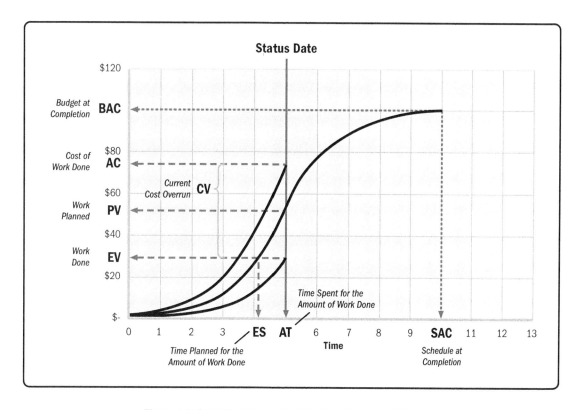

Figure 4-3. Graphical View of the EVM Cost Variance (CV) Metric

Besides being calculated cumulatively, CV can also be calculated periodically to analyze the specific variance that occurred in each time period and its contribution to the total cumulative variance.

4.4.1.2 SCHEDULE VARIANCE

Schedule variance (SV) is a measure that reflects the difference between the amount of work planned to be accomplished and the amount of work actually accomplished at the present time. It answers the following management questions related to time performance:

◆ Is the amount of work performed more or less than planned to date?

◆ Was more or less time spent than planned based on the amount of work accomplished?

◆ How much more or less time was spent than planned?

The amount of work is measured in budget value using the unit of measure selected (see Section 4.3). SV can be expressed in both volume of work (SV_w) or in time (SV_t).

◆ **Schedule variance expressed in volume (SV_w).** When expressed in volume, SV_w is a measure of *work volume variance*. It measures the deficit or the abundance of work accomplishment over time.

The equation used to express schedule variance as of the date of examination is:

$$SV_w = EV - PV$$

When the variance is equal to 0, it means that as much quantity of work has been accomplished as planned (but not necessarily the specific work that was scheduled to be performed). When SV is negative, the work is behind schedule since a lesser quantity of work than planned has been accomplished. Finally, when SV_w is positive, the work is ahead of schedule because a greater quantity of work than planned has been accomplished.

◆ **Schedule variance expressed in time (SV_t).** When expressed in time, SV_t is a measure of time variance. It measures the excess, or the savings of time, consumed with the work accomplished. It is based on the concept of ES.

EVM includes the concept of ES where time is used for measuring schedule variance and performance, instead of using work. Most EVMS use the concept of work volume to measure time performance, as previously described by measuring SV in the budget (Y) axis. Schedule variance can also be measured in the time (X) axis by considering the difference between the time already spent with the amount of work accomplished, and the time (according to the baseline) that was expected to be spent to accomplish the same amount of work (but not necessarily that same work). In this approach, SV_t is a measure of time variance.

The equation used to express schedule variance in this way as of the date of examination is:

$$SV_t = ES - AT$$

When the variance is equal to 0, it means that as much time has been spent as planned to accomplish the quantity of work performed to date (but not necessarily according to schedule). When the SV is negative, the work is behind schedule since more time than planned was necessary to accomplish the current quantity of work performed. Finally, when SV is positive, the work is ahead of schedule since less time than planned was necessary to accomplish the current quantity of work performed.

Both schedule variances can also be expressed in percent relative to the PV and ES:

$$SV_w\% = SV_w/PV = \text{amount of work variance / planned value}$$

$$SV_t\% = SV_t/ES = \text{time variance / earned schedule}$$

◆ **SV_w vs. SV_t.** Both variances are useful for the purpose of variance analysis and response, since they provide complementary information from two different dimensions that matter for the purpose of performance management.

For example, 20% less work was accomplished than the work that was planned to date, and it has taken 1 extra month so far. In this example, $SV_w\% = -20\%$ and $SV_t = -1$ month. Figure 4-4 illustrates these two variances in absolute value.

Both variances are complementary and are useful in assessing the current status of the project regarding time efficiency and performance. The volume-based variance SV_w has been used more widely because it measures the *source* of the variation (i.e., the deficit or abundance of scope realization) as opposed to its *impact* (i.e., the current time variation). Assuming management can intervene to accelerate or decelerate the project's execution, it is the SV_w that should be looked at and considered to calculate the required future execution rate, while SV_t is the measure of the current time impact of the realization deficit or abundance. In scenarios where the scope execution rate cannot be significantly changed (e.g., painting the interior of a very confined space, such as a submarine), SV_t may become more relevant to assess the impacts on the project schedule. For the vast majority of a project's scope, modern working processes and technology provide ways of changing the work execution rate.

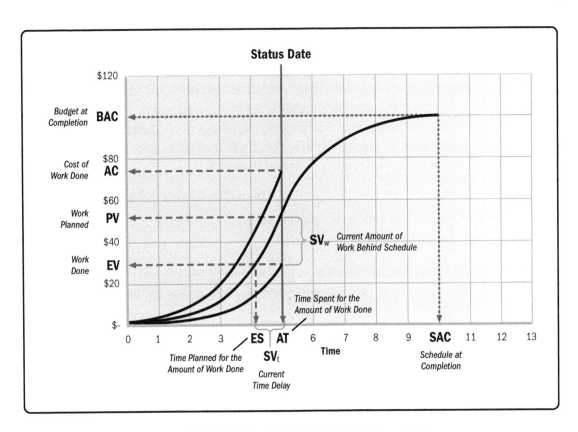

Figure 4-4. Graphical View of the EVM Schedule Variance Metrics

Like CV, SV can also be calculated periodically to analyze the specific variance that occurred in each time period and its contribution to the total cumulative variance. Attention is required, however, when interpreting this periodic analysis in cases when work is performed out of sequence.

4.4.1.3 PERFORMANCE INDICES

Another analysis provided by an EVMS is the measurement of performance indices, based on ratios, which provide complementary information to understand the current performance and its causes, feasibility of objectives, and future trends.

◆ **Cost performance indices (CPI).** A measure of the cost efficiency of budgeted resources expressed as the ratio of EV to actual cost. The following indices can be calculated:

CPI = EV / AC

- CPI equals budget of work accomplished / actual cost of work accomplished.
- CPI measures how much work is being produced for each unit of cost incurred.

For example, when CPI = 0.8, this means that for every 1 unit of cost incurred, only 0.8 of work was accomplished. When cost and budget are measured in monetary value, then for each $1[2] spent on average, only $0.80 of work was produced (over budget). In the baseline, each 1 of cost is expected to produce $1 of work.

TCPI (to-complete CPI) = (BAC − EV) / (BAC − AC)

- TCPI is equal to the amount of work remaining / amount of budget remaining.
- TCPI measures how much work needs to be produced in the future for every unit of cost spent, so that the work is completed on budget (assuming there is still budget available; therefore BAC > AC).

For example, TCPI = 1.2, which means that for the budget remaining, every 1 unit of cost to be spent should produce 1.2 units of work. If cost and budget are measured in monetary value, then on average for each $1 to be spent in the future, $1.20 of work should be produced. TCPI can also be calculated in relation to a potential budget review or new target cost (i.e., a what-if analysis), where an EAC_c (new budget or target cost) replaces BAC in the denominator.

The to-complete performance index assesses the remaining future of the project, providing for a proactive assessment of whether the budget available is sufficient to complete the work and what is the required future efficiency. In a mature organization, benchmarking is available to assess whether certain performance levels above the baseline, as measured by the to-complete performance index, are attainable or whether it is better to consider project changes.

◆ **Schedule performance indices (SPI).** Schedule performance indices provide a measure of efficiency regarding the time consumed with the amount of work accomplished. The following indices can be calculated:

SPI_w (schedule performance index expressed in work volume variance) = EV / PV

- SPI equals the amount of work accomplished / amount of work planned to be accomplished.
- SPI measures, on average, the fraction of work that is being accomplished in each unit of time where 1 unit of work should have been accomplished according to the baseline. SPI measures the actual rate at which the work is being accomplished relative to the expected work rate in the baseline.

For example, SPI = 0.6 means that, on average, for every unit of time where 1 unit of work should have been accomplished, only 0.6 units of work was actually accomplished. The actual work rate is only 60% of what was planned in the baseline; therefore, the work is getting done slower at a 60% rate.

---

[2] All costs in this standard are provided in U.S. dollars.

$TSPI_w$ (to-complete SPI expressed in work volume variance) = (BAC − EV) / (BAC − PV)

- TSPI equals the amount of work remaining / amount of work planned to be remaining;
- TSPI measures how much work needs to be produced in the future for every unit of time where 1 unit of work was planned to be accomplished, so that the work is completed on time. It measures the future work rate required for the time remaining relative to the planned rate for that same period.

For example, TSPI = 1.3 means that for the time remaining, in every unit of time where 1 unit of work was planned to be accomplished, 1.3 units of work need to be accomplished. The future work rate required to complete on time is 130% of the planned rate in the baseline for the time remaining; therefore, the work needs to be done 30% faster. $TSPI_w$ can also be calculated in relation to a potential scope change (i.e., a what-if analysis), where an EAC_c (budget for the modified total scope) replaces BAC in the denominator.

The calculations for SPI and TSPI were based on comparing work volume as measured in the budget (Y) axis of the EVM data points. As with schedule variance (SV), both SPI and TSPI can also be measured in the time (X) axis:

SPI_t (schedule performance index) = ES / AT

- SPI_t equals time planned for the amount of work accomplished / time actually spent for the amount of work accomplished.
- SPI_t measures, on average, the fraction of the time elapsed to accomplish each unit of work.

For example, SPI_t = 0.7 means that only 70% of the time was actually spent with every unit of work accomplished. For example, 10 days are being spent for each unit of work, when only 7 days should have been spent). On average, more time is being spent with each unit of work than planned in the baseline (10 days as opposed to 7); therefore, the work is getting done slower:

$TSPI_t$ (to-complete SPI) = (SAC − ES) / (SAC − AT)

- TSPI equals the amount of time planned for the work remaining / amount of time actually remaining;
- TSPI measures how much time needs to be progressed in the baseline, for each unit of time remaining, so that the work is completed on time. In other words, it measures the future work rate required to accomplish the remaining work relative to the planned rate for that same amount of work.

For example, $TSPI_t$ = 1.5, which means that, on average, for the time remaining, the amount of work that needs to be accomplished corresponds to 1.5 units of time in the baseline. For example, if there are only 10 days remaining to accomplish the remaining work for which 15 days had been planned in the baseline, then the amount of work that now needs to be produced in each remaining day in the baseline will consume 1.5 days.

The future work rate required to complete on time is 150% of the planned rate in the baseline for the same amount of work remaining; therefore, the work needs to be done faster. For example, for every month, the amount of work to be accomplished will consume 1.5 months in the baseline. $TSPI_t$ can also be calculated in relation to a potential schedule change (i.e., a what-if analysis), where an EAC_t (revised duration) replaces SAC in the denominator.

While less intuitive, the use of the time-based schedule performance indices, as an alternative to the traditional volume-based indices for time-performance measurement, has been receiving some attention from a community of EVM practitioners. The main argument is related to the natural tendency of volume-based SPI to float toward 1 when the work is behind schedule beyond the baseline completion date; therefore, it is not a reliable predictor of final variance at completion. However, for forecasting purposes, in such behind-schedule scenarios, the volume-based SPI can be adjusted to deliver consistent and valid future trends.

$$SPI = (EV / PV) \times (SAC / AT)$$

Where: AT > SAC, as the baseline completion date overrun.

TSPI is an important index that assesses the remaining future of the project. It provides a proactive assessment of whether the time remaining is sufficient to complete the work and determines the required future efficiency. Again, in a mature organization, benchmarking is available to assess whether certain performance levels above the baseline, as measured by TSPI, are attainable or whether it is better to consider project changes.

Table 4-1 presents a summary for the formulas of the EVM performance indices.

Table 4-1. Formulas of the EVM Performance Indices

Index	Past	Future
Cost Performance	• $CPI = EV/AC$	$TCPI = (BAC - EV)/(BAC - AC)$ What-if analysis for BAC: $TCPI = (BAC - EV)/(IEAC_c - AC)$

Shedule Performance	• $SPI_w = EV/PV$
	  where: $AT \leq SAC$
	
	• $SPI_w = (EV/PV) \times (SAC/AT)$
	  where: $AT > SAC$
	
	• $SPI_t = ES/AT$
		• $TSPI_w = (BAC - EV)/(BAC - PV)$
		• $TSPI_t = (SAC - ES)/(SAC - AT)$
		
		What-if analysis for BAC and SAC:
		• $TSPI_w = (BAC - EV)/(IEAC_c - PV)$
		• $TSPI_t = (SAC - ES)/(IEAC_t - AT)$

When an organization is mature in using EVM, performance indices are compared against variation thresholds derived from historical data of past projects, which work as control limits. When the performance indices vary within the thresholds, then no corrective action is required. A variation beyond the control limit can be a warning sign that corrective action is recommended to counter the negative performance or to exploit the positive performance being observed. This approach, based on thresholds, can also be used to implement management by exception.

4.4.1.4 POTENTIAL CAUSES OF VARIANCES

Once variances are identified and measured, it is important to diagnose the causes so that, when necessary, action can be taken to either mitigate or enhance their influence over the project.

Effective management does not aim at the absence of variance. Instead, good management is about identifying and measuring variance, understanding its causes, and acting upon them, when required. This is a continuous process where negative variance is treated early to prevent propagation and ripple effects, and where positive variance is exploited as opportunities to improve the project's final performance.

The EVM metrics and indices help to diagnose variation by providing detailed visibility of where the variance is occurring:

◆ Causes for variances can be identified by using the varying levels of the WBS to identify the scope components with the larger variances;

◆ Variances can be calculated on specific segments of the project scope, for example:

■ Scope assigned to specific contractors or functional units,

■ Type of work (e.g., engineering, excavation, programming), and

■ Type of resource engaged in doing the work.

This type of top-down and segmented analysis is useful for understanding where, who, and what type of work is overperforming or underperforming. This analysis focuses the action where it is most needed.

When an organization is mature in using EVM, correlations regarding the status of the project can be established using EVM metrics, performance indices, and potential causes for variance based on historical data and lessons learned. In other words, common symptoms can be consistently linked to potential causes, as shown in Table 4-2.

Table 4-2. Potential Causes for Variance

	SPI < 1 (behind schedule)	SPI > 1 (ahead of schedule)
CPI < 1 **(above budget)**	*Underestimation?* *Unexpected scope complexity?*	*Overresourced?* *Work executed out of sequence?*
CPI > 1 **(below budget)**	*Underresourced?* *Value engineering?*	*Overestimated?* *Scope simpler than expected?* *Effective risk management?*

Once causes are diagnosed, they should be documented for later verification and review. Maintaining an updated record of observed variance and its diagnosis is essential for continuous improvement in order to develop and maintain effective responses. Such records are invaluable, particularly for large future projects to be used for forecasting both at a strategic level and for creating future project estimates. For example, past experience may indicate that certain specific causes of underperformance may persist in the project during certain periods of time and this would affect the calculation of the estimates at completion.

4.4.1.5 POTENTIAL MANAGEMENT ACTIONS

When potential causes are identified and documented, a list of possible actions to conduct an impact analysis should be developed prior to the decision to implement.

An organization using EVM systematically and consistently should be able to:

◆ Develop a knowledge base linking the key three elements of decision making: symptoms, causes, and recommended actions; or

◆ Capture the information into existing organizational decision logs.

When the relationship between causes and effective actions is not supported by objective or consistent empirical evidence, decision making may be limited to less scientific measures, such as general rules of thumb or personal experience and preferences.

A recommended practice is to develop a more systematic approach to the identification of possible actions so as to act upon variations either by mitigating or enhancing their effect on the project. Examples of possible actions are provided in Table 4-3.

Table 4-3. Examples of Possible Actions for Impact Analysis

	SPI < 1 (behind schedule)	SPI > 1 (ahead of schedule)
CPI < 1 (above budget)	*Underestimation?* *Unexpected scope complexity?* Potential actions: • Descope the project • Increase budget/schedule (when TCPI and TSPI are high)	*Overresourced?* *Work executed out of sequence?* Potential actions: • Reduce resources • Rebaseline for early completion • Control work out of sequence
CPI > 1 (below budget)	*Underresourced?* *Value engineering?* Potential actions: • Increase resources • Rebaseline to extend the schedule (if TSPI is very high)	*Overestimated?* *Scope simpler than expected?* *Effective risk management?* Potential actions: • Expand the scope and/or quality • Plan additional risk responses to reduce project risk • Rebaseline for early completion and release budget

Once the potential actions are identified, they should be documented along with the rationale for further analysis regarding the impact on the project.

4.4.2 FORECASTING

As the project progresses, future trends can be developed for cost and schedule performance in addition to scope at completion. These trends should take the form of scenario analysis and incorporate the following elements as impacting the project future:

◆ Past performance,

◆ Occurrence of risks,

◆ Management actions, and

◆ Review of project assumptions and constraints.

Trends are quantified in the form of forecasting EVM data points, which include:

◆ **Estimate to complete (ETC).** The ETC is the expected cost or time needed to complete all of the remaining work for a control account, work package, or project.

There are two possible ways to develop the ETC. The most detailed method is to develop a new bottom-up estimate based on an analysis of the remaining work. This is sometimes referred to as a management ETC.

Another alternative is to use a top-down parametric approach, applying a future efficiency to the remaining work. For cost, such an estimate is calculated as follows:

ETC = work remaining / future expected efficiency = (BAC − EV) / CPI-future

Where CPI-future is the assumed future cost efficiency for the work remaining, for which difference scenarios can be considered:

■ Independent estimate to complete (IETC) assumes no management intervention. Common alternatives for CPI-future are:

○ Future efficiency will be the same as the average observed in the past.

○ Future efficiency is the same as the average observed in the most recent control period (e.g., month, quarter).

○ Future efficiency is based on a trend of the past efficiency (statistically derived).

■ Future efficiency is affected by management intervention and/or occurrences of other events foreseen by management (e.g., risks and risk responses). This results in a change from the past efficiency. If CPI-future becomes equal to TCPI, ETC will be equal to the budget remaining: BAC − AC.

■ Statistical, parametric, or empirical approaches can also be used to extrapolate CPI-future from past performance indices and other factors, with some approaches using a combination of past CPI and SPI.

A similar rationale and approach can be used to estimate the ETC for the time remaining in the project, using the time-efficiency indices.

◆ **Estimate at completion (EAC).** EAC is the expected total cost or time of a control account, work package, or project when the defined scope of work will be completed.

The equation for EAC is the current cost or time spent plus the estimate to complete (ETC):

$$EAC_c = AC + ETC_c$$

$$EAC_t = AT + ETC_t$$

When the independent estimate is used for ETC, then EAC is often referred to as an independent estimate at completion (IEAC).

Different approaches to estimate the cost and time remaining can be used.

◆ **Variance at completion (VAC).** The VAC is the variance between the forecasted trend and the baseline for cost and schedule, and it can be calculated in absolute value or as a percentage over the total:

$$VAC_c = BAC - EAC_c$$

$$VAC_c\% = VAC_c / BAC$$

$$VAC_t = SAC - EAC_t$$

$$VAC_t\% = VAC_t / SAC$$

The VAC shows the trend for the total variation of the project cost and schedule, using scenarios with and without management potential actions. These scenarios of potential variation over the baseline (BAC and SAC) should not be accepted as inevitable alternative outcomes. Instead, the scenarios should be discussed and analyzed to form the basis of management decisions. These decisions may include changing the baseline to accommodate negative performance or to embrace the opportunities of positive performance in accordance with the integrated change process (see Section 4.6 for further details).

Figure 4-5 shows a summary of the EVM trend variances and how they relate to past variance. In this example, it is shown as a negative cost performance that is trending toward partial recovery (i.e., $VAC_c < CV$), with a time delay that is trending to get worse (i.e., $VAC_t > SV_t$).

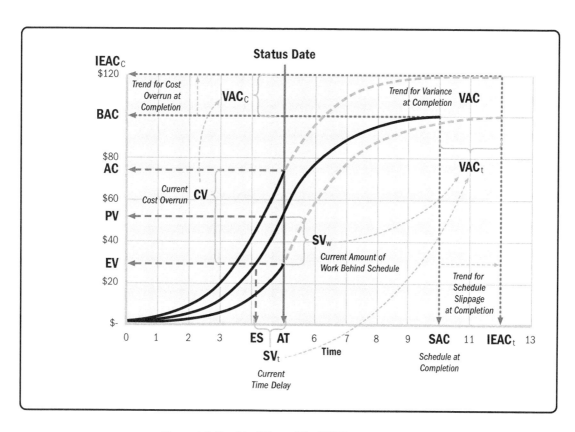

Figure 4-5. Graphical View of the EVM Trend Variances

Additional examples of graphical representations can be found in Appendix X4.

◆ **To-Complete Performance Indices.** Performance indices regarding the future were described in Section 4.4.1.3 as the performance required to complete on budget (TCPI) and on time (TSPI), according to the baseline.

In situations where management is considering scenarios to change the baseline, these indices can be calculated against the new objectives in order to assess whether these are realistic. The equations are the same, with the new objectives for cost and time being used instead of the current baseline (see Figure 4-6).

Project Baseline		Current Status	
		Actual Time (AT) =	5
Budget at Completion (BAC) =	$ 1,000	Planned Value (PV) =	$ 600.00
Schedule at Completion (SAC) =	10	Earned Value (EV) =	$ 400.00
		Actual Cost (AC) =	$ 500.00

Performance Status			
Cost Performance Index (CPI) =	0.8	*Past cost efficiency*	EV/AC
To Complete on Budget CPI (TCPI) =	**1.20**	*Future cost performance required to complete within the approved budget*	(BAC – EV)/(BAC – AC)
IEAC$_c$ – Independent EAC (Cost) =	$ 1,250	*Trend for the final cost at completion assuming past efficiency will continue into the future*	BAC/CPI
VAC$_c$ – Variance at Completion (Cost) =	**$ –250**	*Trend for final cost variation at completion*	BAC – IEAC(c)
Schedule Performance Index (SPI) =	0.67	*Past schedule efficiency*	EV/PV
To Complete on Schedule SPI (TSPI) =	**1.50**	*Future schedule performance required to complete within the approved schedule*	(BAC – EV)/(BAC – PV)
IEAC$_t$ – Independent EAC (Time) =	15	*Trend for the final schedule at completion assuming past efficiency will continue into the future*	SAC/SPI
VAC$_t$ – Variance at Completion (Time) =	**–5**	*Trend for the final schedule duration variation at completion*	SAC – IEAC(t)

Scenario Analysis for Budget Adjustment for the Extra Work			
Budget Adjustment =	$ 150	*The approved budget is increased to accommodate past underperformance*	
New Adjusted Budget (New BAC) =	$ 1,150	*The new total approved budget*	BAC + Budget Adjustment
To Complete on New Budget CPI (TCPI) =	**1.15**	*Future cost performance required to complete within the adjusted budget (New BAC)* *= New Work Remaining/New Budget Remaining*	(New BAC – EV)/(New BAC – AC)

Scenario Analysis for Schedule Adjustment			
Schedule Adjustment =	2	*The approved schedule is increased to accommodate past underperformance*	
New Adjusted Schedule (New SAC) =	12	*The new total approved schedule duration*	SAC + Schedule Adjustment
To Complete on New Schedule SPI (TSPI) =	**1.07**	*Future schedule performance required to complete within the newly adjusted schedule* *= New Work Rate/Original Work Rate = 85.71/80*	[(BAC – EV)/(New SAC – AT)]/[(BAC – PV)/(SAC – AT)]
Original Work Rate Assumed in the Baseline =	$ 80.00	*The original time remaining (i.e., SAC – AT = 5 Time Periods), a work rate of $80.00 per time period was assumed* *= Work Planned Remaining/Time Remaining = ($1,000 – $600/(10 – 5) = $400/5 time periods*	(BAC – PV)/(SAC – AT)
New Work Rate Assumed in the New SAC =	$ 85.71	*In the new time remaining (i.e., New SAC – AT = 7 Time Periods), a work rate of $85.71 per time period is now required* *= Current Work Remaining/New Time Remaining = ($1,000 – $400)/(12 – 5) = $600/7 time periods*	(BAC – EV)/(New SAC – AT)

Scenario Analysis for Schedule and Budget Adjustment for the Extra Work			
New Adjusted Budget (New BAC) =	$ 1,150	*The new total approved budget*	BAC + Budget Adjustment
New Adjusted Schedule (New SAC) =	12	*The new total approved schedule duration*	SAC + Schedule Adjustment
To Complete on New Schedule SPI (TSPI) =	**1.34**	*Future schedule performance required to complete on schedule within the new scenario of schedule and budget adjustment* *= New Work Rate/Baseline Work Rate = 107.14/80.00*	
New Work Rate Assumed in the New BAC and New SAC =	$107.14	*In the new time remaining (i.e., New SAC – AT = 7 Time Periods), a work rate of $107.14 per time period is now required* *= New Work Remaining/New Time Remaining = ($1,150 – $400)/(12 – 5) = $750/7 time periods*	(New BAC – EV)/(New SAC – AT)

Figure 4-6. Example of To-Complete Performance Index for New Objective

Confronted with a scenario of a 5-month potential delay ($IEAC_t$ = 15 months) and a cost overrun of $250 due to emerging extra work, management is considering some replanning actions to complete the project in 12 months (SAC_{new}) and/or allowing for a $150 increase in the budget (BAC_{new}) to cover the cost of extra future work required. Adjusting only the schedule and assuming that no extra work will emerge implies an increase over the baseline work rate by 7% ($TSPI_{new}$ = 1.07), which is far more realistic than trying to complete in 10 months with an unlikely work rate increase of 50% (TSPI = 150%). Assuming that extra future work will emerge and adjusting the budget accordingly, cost efficiency should also be improved but only to 1.15, which is less than 1.20 if this extra work was not accommodated and the budget was not changed. In the scenario where both schedule and budget changes are made to the baseline, this implies a work rate increase of 34% ($TSPI_{new}$ = 1.34), which is still more realistic than a 50% increase with no changes. The required cost and schedule performance variations implied in the management actions are measured in percent against the performance assumed in the current baseline, prior to approving the changes. The EVM to-complete indices provide a means of objective information to assess the feasibility and effectiveness of management actions.

4.4.2.1 SCOPE VARIANCE AND PERFORMANCE

EVM variance metrics and indices consider that the scope is fixed and needs to be accomplished in full. In some cases, the scope is flexible enough to accommodate stricter cost and time objectives.

EVM metrics can be adapted to measure trends in scope variation and final scope performance, depending on past cost and time performance. For example, the trend for scope at percent complete as a function of past CPI and SPI and expected future CPI and SPI, measures the fraction of the original scope that is likely to be accomplished. When greater than 100%, this means that the scope can be potentially enhanced as an opportunity that management may decide to explore.

Conversely, considering a required scope increase, the future pressure on cost and time performance can be calculated in the form of the TCPI and TSPI (future performance) required to accomplish that scope.

4.4.2.2 TREND ANALYSIS

Identifying trends in the performance metrics can help a project manager decipher or anticipate a potential performance problem. For example, a cumulative CPI that is within an acceptable range, but has been trending down toward a preestablished threshold for that index for several measurement periods, may be cause for some concern and prompt an examination of the underlying cause for the trend. When the trend is seen at the project level, the WBS will enable the manager to drill down to lower levels to see what underlies the trend.

The use of the management reserve (MR) may also be monitored on EVMS reports. For example, a large drawdown of the management reserve early in the project may indicate that many unforeseen events have occurred. This may suggest a trend for the inability to resolve unforeseen threats later as the project progresses. Thresholds may be established that would trigger management involvement to investigate when a large percentage of MR is used early in the project. For example, if 50% of MR has been used and the project scope is 20% or less complete, then management should investigate the causes of the MR use. Any large call for additional funding from the MR should lead to a reassessment of project assumptions and reevaluation of the corresponding planning decisions.

4.4.2.3 SUMMARY OF EVM METRICS

Table 4-4 is a collection of the main EVM metrics that can be produced by an EVMS and the important management questions they address.

Table 4-4. Summary of EVM Metrics

EVM Metric	Description	Management Question
Baseline:		
BAC	Budget at completion	What is the currently approved budget?
SAC	Schedule at completion	What is the currently approved schedule?
Current Status:		
PV	Planned value	How much work is planned to be accomplished?
EV	Earned value	How much work has been accomplished?
AC	Actual cost	How much cost has been incurred to date?
ES	Earned schedule	How much time was planned for the amount of work accomplished?
AT	Actual time	How much time has elapsed?
CV	Cost variance	How much is the project overspending or underspending?
SV_w	Schedule variance (work)	How much work is ahead or behind schedule?
SV_t	Schedule variance (time)	How much time is the project ahead or behind schedule?
CPI	Cost performance index	How much work is being accomplished for every unit of currency spent?
SPI_w	Schedule performance index (work)	For the time elapsed, what is the actual work rate against the baseline?
SPI_t	Schedule performance index (time)	For the work done, what is the actual work rate against the baseline?
Future:		
TCPI	To-complete CPI	What is the required future cost performance to complete the project on a specific budget?
TSPI	To-complete SPI	What is the required future time performance to complete the project on a specific time?
IETC	Independent estimate to complete	What is the trend for the cost and time required to complete the project given its past performance?
IEAC	Independent estimate at completion	What is the trend for the final cost and time given its past performance?
ETC	Estimate to complete	What is the cost and time required to complete the project?
EAC	Estimate at completion	What is the trend for the final cost and time given the past performance and management actions?

4.4.3 MANAGING PERFORMANCE WITH EVM FOR AGILE

Enterprises are becoming aware that they do not need to adhere to a single methodology (e.g., predictive or adaptive approaches), which has led to the creation of hybrid concepts (see also Section 3.5). However, the project manager may be responsible for managing several concurrent, high-visibility projects or CAs using a mixture of plan-driven (i.e., predictive) and agile (i.e., adaptive) methods in a fast-paced environment that may cross multiple business divisions.

4.4.3.1 SUPPLEMENTING AGILE REPORTING WITH EVM

Traditional agile metrics (see Section 5.4 of the *Agile Practice Guide*) do not provide (a) estimates of cost at completion of the release or (b) cost metrics to support the business with managing costs to evaluate expected return on investment and other financial information. Therefore, the iteration burndown and release burnup charts (as used in Scrum and other agile approaches) do not provide at-a-glance project cost information. Additionally, agile metrics neither provide estimates of cost at completion of the release nor cost metrics to support the business when they consider making decisions like changing requirements in a release. EVM for agile extrapolates this information and is therefore an excellent extension of the information provided by the agile release burnup charts.

4.4.3.2 CALCULATING PV, EV, AND AC WITHIN AGILE

The comparison of EV with PV lies at the core of EVM. PV is the value of the work planned for a certain date. It is the entire budget for work to be completed at the planned date. In agile terminology: It is the sum of the estimated feature sizes for all the features up until the planned date.

For agile projects or control accounts, EV represents the value of work completed (i.e., total number of story points for all completed user stories times number of completed iterations) at the same date as used for PV. EV is not synonymous with actual cost, nor does the term refer to business value. EV refers to technical performance (work) *earned* or completed against the baseline or work planned. In agile terminology, it is the value of the completed user stories up until the calculation/status date.

Actual cost is what the name implies: the cost in dollars to complete a set of user stories by the team per iteration and is usually derived from work hours recorded by the organization's time reporting/tracking system.

Agile EVM works by comparing the current release plan (taking into consideration changes to the scope in the product backlog) against actual work completed as captured in the release burnup chart. For example, progress can be shown on a burnup chart as depicted in Figure 4-7, where story points are mapped into financial value based on a value-per-point conversion rate of $3,500 per point (i.e., the burn rate). At the end of the R3-S9 timebox, the cumulative EV is less than the cumulative PV. A detailed explanation is provided in Table 4-5 where at the end of the R3-S9 timebox, cumulative EV = 390 points or $1,365K and cumulative PV = 450 points or $1,575K with an actual cost equal to $1,507K. For EVM reporting on a hybrid project, the CPI of 0.91 and SPI of 0.87 for this CA will be included in the consolidated report for the project. See Section 4.5.1.1 for an example of consolidated reporting for a hybrid project.

It is important to note that in agile EVM there is no credit for partial completion. The backlog items are either done or not done (0 or 100%). In keeping with agile terminology, a backlog item is considered to be complete and done when the customer accepts the item.

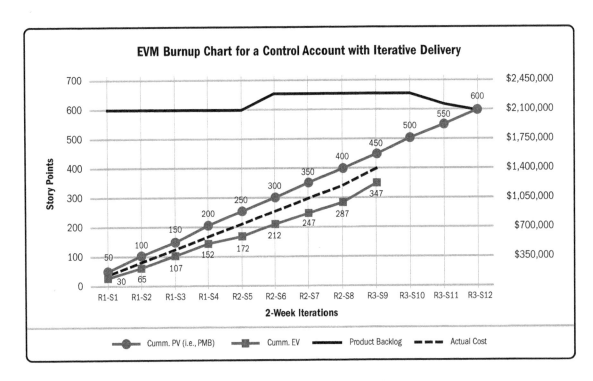

Figure 4-7. Burnup Chart for Agile with EVM

Table 4-5. Details for Burnup Chart for Agile with EVM

Solution Status by Sprint												
RELEASE	R1				R2				R3			
SPRINT	R1-S1	R1-S2	R1-S3	R1-S4	R2-S5	R2-S6	R2-S7	R2-S8	R3-S9	R3-S10	R3-S11	R3-S12
Product Backlog	600	600	600	600	600	650	650	650	650	650	610	590
Planned Value (Target Velocity)[A]	50	50	50	50	50	50	50	50	50	50	50	50
Earned Value (Actual Velocity)[B]	30	35	42	45	20	40	35	40	60			
Remaining Backlog	570	535	493	448	428	388	403	363	303			
Actual Work Performed (Story Points)	40	40	40	43	46	44	46	46	47			
Actual Cost per Iteration ($K)[C]	$140	$140	$140	$15	$160	$155	$160	$160	$165			
Cumulative Actual Work Performed (Story Points)[D]	40	80	120	163	209	253	299	344	391			
Cumulative Actual Work Performed (Cost $K)[E]	$140	$280	$420	$570	$730	$855	$1,045	$1,205	$1,370	$1,370	$1,370	$1,370
Cumulative Planned Value (i.e., PMB)	50	100	150	200	250	300	350	400	450	500	550	600
Cumulative PV ($K)	$175	$350	$525	$700	$875	$1,050	$1,225	$1,400	$1,575	$1,750	$1,925	$2,100
Cumulative Earned Value	30	65	107	152	172	212	247	287	347			
Cumulative EV ($K)	$105	$228	$375	$532	$602	$742	$865	$1,005	$1,215			
AC	$140	$280	$420	$570	$370	$885	$1,045	$1,205	$1,370	$1,370	$1,370	$1,370
CPI	0.75	0.81	0.89	0.93	0.82	0.84	0.83	0.83	0.89			
SPI	0.60	0.65	0.71	0.76	0.69	0.71	0.71	0.72	0.77			

Today's Status Date
(End of R3-S9)

[A] Planned Value (PV) is the budgeted labor cost based on team composition and anticipated velocity derived from historical averages. Assume PV remains constant per iteration during the release.

[B] Earned Value (EV) is the value of completed work expressed as the cumulative velocity from completed iterations compared to the planned value and may be dollarized based on the planned value's labor cost per story points.

[C] Actual Cost (AC) in an agile program is collected the same as any traditional program where actual work done is tracked against charge numbers established for executing specific work scope. However, AC may be influenced by additional overtime work to meet commitments.

[D] Burn Rate or 3.5($K) / Story Point is an average of how many points were delivered over a period of time compared to the labor cost over the same period. The organization may use historical or industry analysis to calculate the burn rate.

[E] It is assumed that the actual cost per iteration is calculated from the organization's time reporting system.

4.4.3.3 BACKLOG IMPACTS ON THE PMB

Agile takes into account that changes to the product backlog may be introduced after each iteration. Changes to the backlog (the added or removed estimated story points caused by added or removed features) effectively rebaselines the plan value after the iteration. The effect of recomputing EVM for agile after every iteration is a validation of the modified backlog against the release plan (i.e., validating that the new scope of work planned for the release is still within schedule and budget goals). This provides the product owner (who owns the backlog) early information about the effects of any changes with enough time to reconsider changes should they negatively affect the release plan. In an agile EVM environment, the PMB equivalent is expressed as "scope of work planned for the release" or *planned value*. This allows for course corrections to be made without disruption or rebaselining of the PMB.

4.4.3.4 FREQUENCY OF MEASUREMENT

Iteration boundaries are well suited to calculate the EVM for agile, although calculations may be made more often depending on the number of iterations in the release or the organization's reporting needs. EVM and agile burnup charts provide important progress status updates for stakeholders. The key consideration is ensuring accurate cumulative values at the reporting boundaries when calculating EVM for agile.

4.4.4 MANAGEMENT DECISION

Decision making occurs when variances in the project have been identified, measured, understood, and documented; and all the relevant potential future scenarios have been identified, quantified, and documented.

The benefits of using EVMS to support decision making stems from the following elements:

◆ Rigor and accuracy, based on valid logic and empirical evidence;

◆ Objectivity, based on the quantification of all aspects of performance;

◆ Auditability, based on EVM's mathematical model and consistency;

◆ Focus, on the relevant aspects of project performance;

◆ Realism, by measuring required future performance; and

◆ Flexibility and capacity, to support a wide range of what-if analysis.

Using EVM therefore increases the likelihood for feasible and effective decisions to be devised and supported by all stakeholders.

It is essential that all stakeholders involved in the decision-making process have sufficient knowledge and understanding of EVM, and share the proactive, rational, transparent, and open management culture upon which it is based. The project team should address how to use EVM information when some of these conditions are not met, in order to prevent negative reactions.

The process of analyzing performance and making final decisions should be documented and subjected to traceability. Observed variance, identified causes, potential actions, trends and forecasts, and final decisions should be recorded and linked to specific timings and stakeholders' responsibilities and accountability.

4.4.4.1 MANAGEMENT BY EXCEPTION

EVM provides an organization with the capability of practicing management by exception on its projects. This practice contributes greatly to the efficiency and effectiveness of project management, by allowing managers and others to focus on project execution and invoke control actions only when and where they are needed. EVM performance measures, used in conjunction with the project work breakdown structure (WBS) and the control thresholds, provide the objective data needed to practice management by exception.

Using EVM, an organization can establish acceptable levels of performance for a project and its work tasks. Variance percentages and efficiency indices are most often used. For example, an organization may consider a CV of plus or minus 10% from the EV to be an acceptable range of variance. For reporting purposes, some organizations color code these performance thresholds. This in no way suggests that an increasing variance should not and could not be dealt with until it crosses the threshold. The thresholds generally define formal reporting parameters. While a negative variance is potentially problematic, a positive variance may represent an opportunity.

Because EVM is usually measured at the control account level where the scope, schedule, and cost of work are planned and controlled, management by exception also starts at this level. EVM performance measures are used to determine whether variance thresholds have been exceeded.

4.5 STAKEHOLDER AND COMMUNICATION CONSIDERATIONS

For the most part, project success depends on effective communications and on managing stakeholders effectively. The Project Communications Management and Project Stakeholder Management Knowledge Areas in the *PMBOK®* *Guide* address best practices and associated processes for project management. The use of EVM has the tremendous potential to support and enhance communications and stakeholder management in projects.

4.5.1 REPORTING

The project team is frequently held accountable for (a) explaining the status of a project that uses EV data and (b) making forecasts as to the probable project outcomes. Often this entails explaining the cost, schedule, and at-completion variances. When communicating variances, it is important that the team describes the cause, impact, and any corrective actions associated with these variances. Responsibility for managing the corrective actions should be assigned to the responsible manager, and the status of corrective actions identified in the past should be addressed. The role of the project sponsor using the performance metrics described previously is important. The project sponsor is responsible for obtaining prompt approval from project governance for the application of corrective actions based on performance metrics.

EVM provides a great deal of useful information to key stakeholders about a project. However, the level and type of information needed about a project varies from one stakeholder to another. For example, the client, owner, or upper management requires a top-line or project-level summary report that indicates whether a project is on time and within budget. By contrast, the project manager needs more detail in order to make any necessary adjustments to the project. Graphs of variance and efficiency data are helpful tools in communicating EV analytics. Computer software, especially when developed specifically for project management and EVM, is effective for producing such graphs.

There are several tools that can be used to present EVM data. These tools are designed to address diverse stakeholder needs. The set of chosen tools and templates for the format of the project reports should be agreed upon by the relevant stakeholders and defined up front in the project management plan. Several of these tools may be used on a given project to meet the needs of different stakeholder audiences. This short list of presentation tools is not, by any means, all encompassing. Other tools such as pie charts, dials, scatter diagrams, and radar or bullseye charts, have all been used and can be very effective methods of conveying EVM information. The most commonly used tools are:

◆ **Tables.** A tabular format is an effective way to display EVM results by project component. A tabular format provides the project manager and other top-level stakeholders with a complete, concise picture of what is happening with each major component of the project. It can be used as a logical follow-up to an S-curve to provide more detail on where the project is at any given point in time.

◆ **Bar charts.** Bar charts can be useful for comparing data such as PV to EV, or AC to EV, and so forth.

◆ **Curves.** S-curves illustrate the cumulative performance metrics of EVM. The typical S-curve is displayed on an X–Y axis with time shown on the X axis and the cost of resources consumed shown on the Y axis. This type of display can be effective for providing a quick look at the overall performance of an activity, control account, or project.

Usually such presentations, particularly the latter, are included in the project performance dashboard regularly communicated to stakeholders. Examples can be found in the example in Appendix X4.

4.5.1.1 EVM REPORTING FOR THE HYBRID PROJECT

When using agile approaches, an organization still needs to achieve the benefit of managing sets of projects in a coordinated manner and to ensure that all projects and control accounts are aligned to key business objectives. It is important that management at all levels is able to see progress measured, risks managed, and the wider view across the project portfolio maintained.

When project teams are comparable in size and velocity, the EVM for agile calculations can be made over the entire project. In a hybrid project, the project teams are not comparable as they work on different parts of the project using different methodologies and different approaches for tracking progress and project costs. Therefore, for hybrid projects, each project team should calculate EVM metrics and then provide a consolidated report for EVM. Table 4-6 shows an EVM report based on the example in Appendix X4. The project has four project teams that use unique control accounts. The CPI and EAC are useful indicators of how the project is doing overall as well as at each CA. In this example, CA-004, Smart Building Information System, has started 3 weeks early; the SPI looks good at 2.80, but the overall project SPI is at 1.15. The project-level SPI is likely a better indicator of the overall project schedule's progress. The project team should review the schedule itself to make a better assessment. For more detail, review the example in Appendix X4.

Table 4-6 shows the summary information from the example in Appendix X4 for the report period ending week 44. With a project CPI of 1.01, the overall project's final cost is forecasted to end comfortably within the accepted cost variance threshold as CA-001, Project Management, has a cost underrun of $10,324. More details can be found in Appendix X4.

Table 4-6. Consolidated Reporting for Hybrid Project

Control Account	Budget at Completion	Planned Value (to date)	Earned Value (to date)	Actual Cost (to date)	Actual Time (Weeks)	Earned Schedule (Weeks)	CPI	SPI$_w$	Estimate to Complete	Estimate at Completion	Cost Variance	Schedule Variance$_t$ (Weeks)
CA-001 Project Management	$336,000	$206,470	$206,470	$216,794	44	44	0.95	1.00	$136,007	$352,801	-$10,324	0
CA-002 Smart Building Planning Phase	$67,700	$67,700	$67,700	$54,057	44	44	1.25	1.00	$0	$54,057	$13,643	0
CA-003 Building Construction	$878,080	$260,283	$324,786	$324,786	44	45	1.00	1.25	$553,294	$878,080	$0	1
CA-004 Smart Building Information System (Agile Team)	122 (Story Points) $61,280	17 (Story Points) $8,336	46 (Story Points) $23,316	$23,316	44	45	1.00	2.80	$37,964	$61,280	$0	1
Program Totals	$1,343,060	$542,789	$622,272	$618,953	44	45	1.01	1.15	$727,265	$1,346,218	$3,319	1

4.5.2 OTHER EXTERNAL COMMUNICATIONS

EVM is an effective tool for generating the information to communicate with stakeholders external to the project team and performing organization.

The project team needs to (a) monitor and align stakeholders' expectations, (b) negotiate planning and project changes, and (c) monitor the performance of work accomplished by suppliers, partner organizations, or resources that are outside of their direct control and authority.

The power and ability of the project team to exert positive and constructive influence over stakeholders and contribute to project success is enhanced with the ability to:

◆ Know (with rigor and accuracy) the true status of the work performed by external entities and stakeholders, and

◆ Anticipate the likely outcomes and alternatives for work in an objective and auditable manner.

For example, EVM to-complete indices can be used to (a) identify unrealistic promises and commitments (often well intended) that are put forward by suppliers or project teams and (b) negotiate and plan for realistic ways to accommodate adversity and explore opportunities. Committing to unrealistic recovery plans as the project unfolds and variations emerge is a common mistake and a poor practice that leads to project failure.

EVM data and information can be used to establish contractual performance obligations and incentives with suppliers, sponsors, and clients and to establish performance appraisal targets for team members.

Once again, the project team should make every effort to involve all external stakeholders at a minimum level in the EVMS. Involving all stakeholders should enable them to trust the information the project team produces and to accept negotiations based on this information.

4.6 INTEGRATED CHANGE CONTROL

The PMB is the integrated plan against which project performance is measured. The PMB is maintained by project management, and it is altered only in accordance with the integrated change process outlined within the project management plan. Figure 3-4 in Section 3.3 displays the PMB relative to its subordinate elements. The relationship of the elements shown to the PMB is addressed in Section 3.3.2.2.

As the project unfolds over time, the project management plan is refined in more detail, and as reserves are used and converted into work scope and resources, the PMB is maintained to accurately reflect the expected project outcome as formally approved by the stakeholders. Implementing integrated change control is a formal process for evaluating these project changes, as outlined in Section 4.6 of the *PMBOK® Guide*. All of the Perform Integrated Change Control processes from the *PMBOK® Guide* are used in EVM. An EVMS can provide enhanced inputs toward data analysis and decision making during the integrated change control process. Changes are documented and formally submitted as requests. Changes are then assessed, and either refused, deferred, or authorized. The decision is recorded and communicated in a disciplined and timely manner. In order to make EVM effective over the span of the entire project, the PMB should be updated to reflect approved change requests before they are implemented.

4.6.1 CHANGE REQUESTS

Change requests may result from project performance, an error in defining the scope of the project or product, evolving requirements, a customer request, a change to a contract, a shift in the regulatory environment, a change in funding, a change in the market, or the occurrence of a risk event (whether foreseen or not). Changes to the PMB may occur when the existing cost, schedule, or scope is no longer realistic.

Changes that are approved are implemented, and the corresponding project management plan components, PMB, and project documents are updated. Changes that are deferred or not approved are recorded in the change log along with the reason for the decision. Effective change management requires disciplined records to carefully control changes to the project and maintain the integrity of the PMB so that measurements are meaningful. Figure 4-8 provides an example of the type of information that could be recorded in a change log about a change request. This is an example and is not inclusive of all information that could be included in a change log.

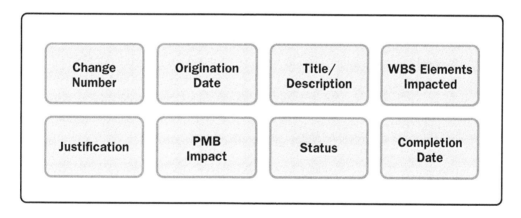

Figure 4-8. Change Log Example Information for a Change Request Affecting the Baseline

4.6.2 CHANGE ANALYSIS

Changes to the project or product scope impact the resources, schedule, and cost of a project. The change control process should account for the analysis that a scope change entails. Changes that do not impact the scope, such as changes to the schedule or the costs, still impact the PMB. The change control process needs to ensure that the integrity of the integrated baseline is not compromised because of these changes or due to external dependencies that these changes impact.

A change control board (CCB) is frequently used to analyze the impact of scope, schedule, cost, and other types of changes on the project and the PMB. The only changes that are implemented are those that are approved by the change control board. On small projects, the project manager may act as the CCB.

4.6.2.1 SCOPE CHANGE ANALYSIS

All scope changes should be analyzed, the scope should be defined, and the impact on the CAs should be assessed. In addition, the need to add new or delete existing CAs should also be determined. Not all changes to the scope result in a cost or schedule impact; however, given the integrated nature of the PMB, it is probable that a scope change will impact the other two areas.

When the scope of the project is changed, such as adding new scope, the PMB should be changed at the WBS level where the scope change occurs.

When new work is added to the CA, the new work should be placed into one or more new work or planning packages. When an existing WP needs to be modified, it should first be closed, then the remaining budget plus new budget should be placed in a new WP. In the latter case, when closing the CA, make the current budget (i.e., the cumulative-to-date PV) equal to EV. This eliminates the schedule variance (i.e., no work remaining to be accomplished in the CA), but the CV is maintained at whatever value it has. Actual costs should not be changed for a CA that is closed due to a scope change. Preserving this cost information maintains the historical CV, which contributes to the project's overall CV. The cumulative PV cannot be changed without changes to the scope and corresponding budget. Cumulative AC or EV cannot be changed either, except to correct prior errors.

Work scope, when moved from one CA to another, is always moved together with its corresponding budget since each budget allocation is authorized specifically for the WBS element to which it is assigned. This maintains the integrity of the PMB. Budget should never be transferred to eliminate variances as this undermines the reporting metrics and jeopardizes effective monitoring and control.

Often when scope changes occur, new CAs are created. When new scope is added, consider whether additional management reserves (MRs) or contingency reserves (CRs) are needed. An analysis of new risks associated with the additional scope may be performed. How these reserves are treated relative to the PMB is addressed in Section 3.3.2.2. Although less frequent, it is possible for the project to be descoped through the change control process.

There are some applications of EVM where contractual requirements create situations in which the customer may initiate a change that needs to be incorporated into the project immediately. The work should be authorized, planned, and executed prior to negotiations on the pricing or cost for the change request. These types of customer-initiated changes are referred to as authorized but unnegotiated changes. In these circumstances, the original contract or a customer-issued letter with a *not-to-exceed* (NTE) amount should indicate how to manage this type of requested change. The portion of the authorized but unnegotiated scope, which can begin immediately, is distributed directly to the CA, and the PMB is modified. Typically, the bulk of the scope identified is for work not yet begun for downstream CAs and WPs. In these cases, the remaining scope and associated value from the NTE letter are held in a higher-level undistributed budget (UB) account. UB accounts should be resolved as quickly as possible, and the proposed scope provided in an NTE letter should be negotiated as soon as practical.

When scope is added or deleted, the WBS and WBS dictionary should be updated to reflect the change in scope. The risk register, cost management plan, and scope management plan may need to be examined and updated accordingly.

4.6.2.2 COST AND SCHEDULE CHANGE ANALYSIS

It is possible to have changes that do not impact the project scope but still impact the cost and/or the schedule—these will have an impact on the PMB. For example, make-or-buy decisions related to the project procurement strategy could cause changes in the cost or schedule that are best incorporated into the PMB. All changes should be analyzed, and the impact on the CAs should be assessed. As mentioned previously, when implementing scope changes, the maintenance of historical variances is required, and the elimination of variances is prohibited except to correct prior errors in reported data.

When cost and schedule are changed, the project management plan and associated project documents may need to be examined and updated accordingly.

4.6.3 REBASELINING

Rebaselining refers to updating the PMB as a result of any approved changes to the schedule, cost, or project scope. A rebaseline equates to a required realignment of the PMB. The desired result from a rebaseline is to improve the integration of the cost, scope, and schedule baselines. To be useful, the PMB should represent a realistic project management plan with attainable objectives. Managing performance against an obsolete baseline is of no value to project monitoring and control.

The rebaseline takes one of two forms:

◆ **Replanning.** Replanning involves a realignment of the remaining schedule and/or a realignment of the remaining budget to meet the original target.

◆ **Reprogramming.** Reprogramming is a comprehensive effort to revamp the PMB. The result of this activity is an over-target baseline (OTB) or over-target schedule (OTS). An OTB includes additional budget in excess of the original budget allocation. An OTS occurs when the scheduled work and the associated budgets are time phased beyond the original completion date.

The OTB is an acknowledgment that the current PMB cannot be executed within the current project constraints. Essentially, cost and schedule objectives have become unattainable such that a secondary baseline should be used to provide meaningful measurement metrics.

The OTB is an attempt to attain project performance objectives in the context of new cost parameters. However, unless the causes for the CVs are identified and rectified, the OTB will not be effective. All parties should focus on the conditions that led to the CVs and agree on the proper corrective actions to take. In some cases, this may be recognition that the original cost objectives were unrealistic. For example, it is possible that the original estimates did not account for the risk component of the estimate.

The OTS acknowledges that the current schedule is unattainable and cannot be executed within the timeframes required. The OTS is an attempt to attain the project performance objectives in the context of new schedule parameters. However, unless the causes for the schedule variances are identified and rectified, the OTS will not be effective. All parties should focus on the conditions that led to the schedule variances and agree on the proper corrective actions to take. In some cases, this may confirm that the original schedule objectives were unrealistic.

The result of any of the previous actions described in this section is a new PMB. As explained earlier, replanning and reprogramming should only modify the baseline information corresponding to future status and actions. Rebaselining should not hide any of the issues experienced in the project up to this point. Once the rebaseline is completed, it needs to be formally approved, communicated, and accepted.

4.7 PROCESS IMPROVEMENT

The continuous improvement of the EVMS is the process of performing constant enhancements to the system through self-evaluation, application learning, and adapting as the project and organizational environment changes. Figure 4-9 shows an example of the evolution of this process.

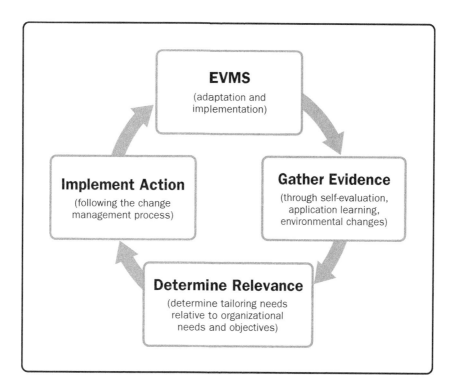

Figure 4-9. Process Improvement Evolution of EVMS

Changes to the EVMS during the execution of a project are almost always inevitable. The system owner should expect requirements to evolve as the projects change and the use of the system matures. Improvements to the EVMS can result from different stimuli and address different aspects of the system, for example:

◆ Stimuli to EVMS continuous improvement:

- Difficulties in collecting data in a timely manner and with quality;
- Difficulties in engaging stakeholders or stakeholders' negative reactions;

- Process delays;
- Communication problems;
- Perceived mismatch between performance information and project reality;
- Changes in project priorities across scope components or objectives (e.g., time vs. cost); and
- Seeking to improve the efficiency and functionalities offered by the system.

◆ Aspects of the EVMS that can be changed:

- Overall process workflow and its activities;
- Procedures, tools, and techniques to be used;
- Roles and responsibilities; and
- Supporting information system and software.

Evaluating both effectiveness and efficiency of the system can be performed through periodic system surveillance (possibly embedded within the established project control cycle) and focus groups where members using the system provide opinions and recommendations. Depending upon the organizational or customer requirements, the frequency with which the surveillance process occurs and the rigor applied can vary. The inclusion of an evaluation process to allow for continuous improvement should be incorporated within the system documents.

EVM is most effective when the system is tailored to suit each project's specific performance management environment, objectives, and goals. For example, the management of an internal project is significantly different from the management of a contract-based project. Likewise, a construction project has significantly different management requirements from a software development project. Care should be taken to profile the EVM requirements to the individual situation during initiating and planning. Later, continued functionality and benefits should be verified as the system and its subsequent metrics are used during project execution.

As the EVMS matures and changes over time and with the implementation of continuous improvements, the project change management processes should be followed. These processes are intended to ensure that changes are incorporated into the system in an organized manner, with the required approvals, and communications to stakeholders are provided in an adequate and timely manner.

5

CLOSING

The Closing Process Group consists of the processes performed to formally complete or close a project, phase, or contract.

5.1 OVERVIEW

Close Project or Phase is the process of finalizing all activities for the project, phase, or contract (see Section 4.7 of the *PMBOK® Guide*). When a project or phase using earned value management (EVM) is closed, EVM is used to finalize information related to the performance measurement baseline (PMB) and assess how work was performed against the overall plan. The project management plan should be reviewed to ensure that the planned work is completed, the project has met its objectives, and project information is archived.

5.2 INCORPORATING EVM INTO PROJECT CLOSEOUT

When performing closing project activities, incorporating data gathered throughout the project by use of the earned value management system (EVMS) allows for full documentation of the baseline execution and change control through completion and project delivery. Aspects of this information, such as summarization of the project's performance and changes over time, should be included in the final report generated as part of the process for Close Project or Phase. Table 5-1 describes some of the main activities of project closeout, as outlined in the *PMBOK® Guide*, along with the impacts and benefits of the use of EVM when performing these activities.

Table 5-1. EVM in Project Closeout Activities

Closeout Activity	Potential Use of EVM	Benefits of EVM
1) Formalize acceptance of delivered scope	Progress metrics and performance indices may be used to demonstrate that acceptance is the best option and/or is according to the objectives	A more objective and auditable demonstration of the scope accomplished and trade-offs of closing the phase or projects makes it easier to reach consensus among the stakeholders
2) Update all project documentation	EVM performance indices and change control information can be used to provide the most accurate information related to project completion of scope, cost, and schedule	Reflects more accurately the actual project execution and completion when archiving projects, and the study of EVM metric trends provides inputs to future decision making
3) Provide team performance assessment	EVM performance indices can be used to provide feedback and calculate key performance indicators (KPIs) segmented by project team (e.g., average CPI of work packages in which the team participated)	A more objective and auditable way to provide feedback to the team and establish performance incentives is more likely to stimulate the team to strive for improvement
4) Evaluate and document the level of project success	Progress metrics and performance indices may be used to better assess impacts of risk and uncertainty realized during project execution on project success (e.g., delivery of project within cost, schedule, and scope parameters)	Improved documentation of project risk and uncertainty leads to better indicators of potential project issues and more accurate estimates
5) Develop and document lessons learned	EVM metrics and indices provide for a better diagnosis of the causes of overperformance or underperformance	A better understanding of variations based on quantitative assessment leads to richer recommendations for better management in the future
6) Update organizational project assets (OPAs)	Use of EVM metrics as indications of trends during execution and auditing during closeout for success or failure based on organizational influences	A better understanding of needed improvements and updates of policies and procedures, growth of corporate knowledge, innovations, and better management of future projects
7) Develop and update the project archive	Progress metrics provide indications of trends during execution for better root cause diagnosis of variances	More objective and auditable historical data for use in future phases and projects allow for better estimates
8) Communicate to stakeholders the project termination and release the project team	Progress metrics and performance indices may be used to communicate effective completion of contractual agreements when the project is complete according to the objectives	A more objective and auditable demonstration of the scope accomplished allows for easier claims management when releasing subcontractors

Each element of the integrated baseline (scope, cost, and schedule) should be evaluated and documented during the closeout process. From an EVM perspective, scope closeout should be documented with a formal acceptance of deliverables and attainment of objectives related to the work breakdown structure (WBS) and the subsequent WBS dictionary. Variances from the project baseline should be documented. The satisfactory completion of scope translates to schedule and cost closeout. Schedule completion is typically achieved with documentation of planned versus actual milestones when generated by the project. Cost closeout should include the collection of all actuals compared to the plan, termination of active cost codes, documentation of completed control accounts, and closure of contracts (includes finalizing open claims). Each element of information should be collected and archived for future use, along with documentation of performance measurement records, significant variances, corrective actions taken, risks encountered, and lessons learned. When an estimating database is used by the organization, the information collected during this time should be processed to update the database. EVM could also be useful in rating and evaluating the staff, vendors, consultants, contractors, and/or other third-party members for future hire. All project-related information should be archived for future use.

Just as each element of the integrated baseline and project success or failure should be evaluated during the closure process, so should the EVMS. Section 4.7 covers incorporating improvements as the EVMS is used during project execution; this should be revisited at the closure of a project. Suggestions for improving and updating the EVMS should be collected through the engagement of project stakeholders at all levels, with users and customers alike.

Building from its continuous improvement during project execution, the EVMS should also be subjected to some important closeout activities. These include and can be coordinated with the process owner:

◆ Evaluate the effectiveness of the EVMS—ease of use, timeliness, effort required, and value of information delivered, among other aspects;

◆ Evaluate the effectiveness of the participants in the EVMS and, where needed, identify further training and communication requirements;

◆ Review roles and responsibilities of the EVMS participants;

◆ Analyze how a phase change (e.g., from engineering to construction) may imply changes or adjustments to the EVMS;

◆ Devise and agree to improvement changes to the EVMS for implementation in the following phase and/or recommendations for future projects; and

◆ Formally close the use of the EVMS for this phase or the total project.

The use of EVM in a project has a positive impact on all activities, enhancing their quality and effectiveness, and thereby contributing to better project management and project performance.

5.3 KNOWLEDGE MANAGEMENT OF EARNED VALUE (EV)

Knowledge management is increasingly important for the transfer of information to target audiences so that institutional knowledge is not lost as the workforce changes (see Section 4.4 of the *PMBOK® Guide*). The purpose of this is so that prior organizational knowledge is leveraged to produce or improve project outcomes and contribute to organizational learning. EVM information enhances an organization's knowledge management system.

As information is gathered during process improvement, as identified in Section 4.7, learning continually evolves throughout the project execution and concludes with reflection during data gathering for project or phase closure (see Section 5.2). This information should be used to update the organizational knowledge base relative to the performance and use of the EVMS on the project. This can be accomplished through compiling lessons learned, management of variances, analysis of trends, and documentation of risks encountered into a database or other forms of documentation for future use. Identifying and sharing patterns that relate to project performance, responses, and their impacts fosters a more robust EVMS. Additionally, knowledge should be shared through interactions with people within the organization (meetings, working groups, etc.) and not only through documentation. When a project management office (PMO) and/or a project management information system (PMIS) exists, as mentioned in Section 1.7, the knowledge gathered should be provided as part of a constant feedback loop. Ultimately, the knowledge gathered will affect updates to the organization's knowledge management system. This process creates ties to decision making, policy creation, and project team management through the use of existing knowledge and creating new knowledge.

A primary goal of applying EVM is to help the project to perform better through improved management. More broadly, the EVMS provides a vital organizational process asset (OPA) at the organizational level for project management organizational learning. Knowledge has two related dimensions: (1) how to better manage the projects, and (2) how to better use EVM via the EVMS. The latter is the basis for the former. For example, an organization can learn from historical data gathering when a control account (CA) or project is overrunning with a to-complete performance index (TCPI) greater than 1.2 (for more on TCPI, see Section 4.4.1.3). In this case, it is more beneficial either to review the budget or to descope the project, rather than to insist on trying to attain the original objectives. In this example, past project data could have shown that trying to attain the original objectives would lead to risky quality cuts and to severe problems during the final project phase or after product delivery.

Working in a hybrid project environment can provide additional opportunities to learn, improve, and create processes, templates, and tools to be more successful. Using lessons learned from an agile retrospective allows for the determination of improvement opportunities across the entire hybrid project. For example, an organization could learn from historical data gathering that before the first 15% to 20% of the planned features are completed, the reported cost performance index (CPI) and schedule performance index (SPI) may not be an accurate indicator of issues, risks, and forecast. As a direct result of this historical knowledge, the organization may not raise "red flags" during first 15% to 20% of the program completion.

In these hybrid environments, historical information may further be of value by contributing to:

◆ Setting up a central team to manage training and oversee and/or manage the transition to agile approaches for other applicable areas based on successful past experiences and to stay relevant with emerging practices.

◆ Creating a Community of Practice (CoP), which may include a pool of trainers, agile coaches, scrum masters, adaptive project managers, predictive project managers, and others who take on full responsibilities in key projects. The existence of a CoP becomes even more relevant for large, complex, and geographically disbursed organizations.

Regardless of the environment, generic management policies can be derived from and improved by empirical evidence with practical experience. When done informally, these generic management policies are called rules of thumb or common practices. The application of EVM provides for a more data-driven approach to establishing these policies, which then constitutes decision-making quality standards. This is just one example on how knowledge elicited by the use of EVM may lead to improved project management policies.

Knowledge sharing (dissemination and accessibility) and integration (from different perspectives and domains) is critical to continuous improvement of the EVMS. This process leads to an effective and appropriately tailored system best suited to the organization's specific performance management environment, objectives, and goals.

APPENDIX X1
DEVELOPMENT OF *THE STANDARD FOR EARNED VALUE MANAGEMENT*

X1.1 OVERVIEW

The *Practice Standard for Earned Value Management – Second Edition* was published in 2011. In 2017, the PMI Standards Manager and the Standards Member Advisory Group chartered the development of a principle-based standard to reflect the core principles and practices for earned value management. In addition, *The Standard for Earned Value Management* is being processed as an ANSI standard.

To fully understand the changes that have been made to the structure and content of *The Standard for Earned Value Management*, it is important for the reader to be aware of the update committee's objectives as well as the evolution of the standard (see Section X1.2).

X1.2 OBJECTIVES

Specifically, the committee's objectives included:

◆ Broadening of the project delivery landscape, including the maturation and adoption of techniques that are, in many cases, better suited to the needs of the modern project manager.

◆ Aligning the document structure with the *PMBOK® Guide* Process Groups to clarify the important considerations from an earned value management (EVM) perspective in that context.

◆ Ensuring that the voice and structure of the standard enables the project team to understand the options and opportunities available to them to define the most appropriate EVM approach to position the project for success.

◆ Ensuring that the updates are harmonized with other PMI standards as appropriate.

X1.3 APPROACH

The document was structured to align with the five major project management Process Groups in the *PMBOK® Guide*. The committee's intent in doing so is to provide a clear line of sight to the *PMBOK® Guide* and the *Agile Practice Guide* when formulating the project approach to EVM.

X1.4 OVERVIEW OF SECTIONS

The standard was arranged in five sections (refer to Sections X1.4.1 through X1.4.5).

X1.4.1 SECTION 1—INTRODUCTION

Section 1 provides an executive overview and perspective of EVM and the value proposition that it offers to help the project team optimize the planning and delivery of their projects. The inclusion of agile and hybrid considerations in addition to the traditional predictive (waterfall) context is explicitly stated, and the guiding principles that underpin the standard are defined. The use of EVM for portfolios and programs is introduced while emphasizing projects as the primary subject of the standard.

X1.4.2 SECTION 2—INITIATING

Section 2 outlines the EVM considerations when the project is operating in the Initiating Process Group. Examples here include identification of the stakeholders, project charter considerations, appropriateness and applicability for a given project, tailoring, and deployment.

X1.4.3 SECTION 3—PLANNING

This section evolves the thought processes outlined in the Planning Process Group to include those considerations that are needed for a successful EVM implementation. Key considerations include developing the project plan, developing and integrating the associated baselines, and establishing the performance measurement baseline. The emphasis is on a disciplined approach to project planning, and the thoughtful integration of planning details into the performance measurement baseline. Risk assessment and management is addressed as a planning and integration consideration. Incorporating the planning process for EVM in an agile/hybrid environment is introduced, as is the concept of earned schedule.

X1.4.4 SECTION 4—EXECUTING, MONITORING, AND CONTROLLING

The Executing and Monitoring and Controlling Process Groups are both addressed in Section 4. The primary emphases in this section are on the project execution processes that are integral to an EVM implementation, and the performance analysis, baseline change control, and project forecasting aspects. Agile/hybrid considerations are also addressed here. The importance of management decision making informed by quantitative data analysis is addressed, as are the stakeholder management and communications aspects of the project management process.

X1.4.5 SECTION 5—CLOSEOUT

The use of EVM in the project management and governance contexts introduces additional project closeout activities, which are discussed in Section 5. Topics including process improvement, assessing EVMS effectiveness in enhancing project delivery, and knowledge management considerations are addressed here.

APPENDIX X2
CONTRIBUTORS AND REVIEWERS OF
THE STANDARD FOR EARNED VALUE MANAGEMENT

This appendix lists, within groupings, those individuals who have contributed to the development and production of *The Standard for Earned Value Management*.

The Project Management Institute is grateful to all of these individuals for their support and acknowledges their outstanding contributions to the project management profession.

X2.1 *THE STANDARD FOR EARNED VALUE MANAGEMENT* CORE COMMITTEE

The following individuals served as members, were contributors of text or concepts, and served as leaders with the core committee:

Cathleen Bischoff Lavelle, MBA, PMP
Larkland A. Brown, SPC4
Panos Chatzipanos, PhD, Dr Eur Ing
John D. Driessnack, CSM, PfMP
Jennifer Fortner, Vice Chair
John C. Post, MBA, PMP, Chair
Alexandre Rodrigues, PhD, PMP
Charles R. Mahon, PMP
Kristin L. Vitello, CAPM, Product Specialist

X2.2 SIGNIFICANT CONTRIBUTOR

In addition to the members of the core committee, the following individual provided significant input to the draft:

Eric Christoph

X2.3 REVIEWERS

X2.3.1 SME REVIEW

The following individuals were invited subject matter experts (SMEs) who reviewed the draft and provided recommendations through the SME review.

Vanita Ahuju, PhD, PgMP

Neil F. Albert

Eric Christoph

Etienne Cornu, PhD, PMI-RMP, PMP

José D. Esterkin, PMP

Connie F. Figley, LEED AP, PMP

Gary M. Hamilton, PMP, PgMP

Suhail Iqbal, PgMP, PfMP

Susan M. Irwin, PhD, PMP

Shirley M. Kelly MSc, PMP

Konstantinos Kirytopoulos, PhD, PMP

Kelly Krug, PMP

Vanina Mangano, PMP

Marcelo Marques, PMI-RMP, PMP

Ken Nishi

Adilson Pize, PMO-CC, PMP

David W. Ross, PMP, PgMP

Salman Shahid, PMI-RMP, PMP

Langeswaran Supramaniam, FCABE C
Build E, PMP

Nathan Subramaniam, ITIL v3 Expert, PMP

Grzegorz Szalajko, CISA, PMP

Gerhard J. Tekes, PMOVR-CP, PMP

Dave Violette, MPM, PMP

X2.3.2 PUBLIC EXPOSURE DRAFT REVIEW

In addition to members of the Core Committee, the following individuals provided recommendations for improving the public exposure draft of *The Standard for Earned Value Management*:

Majed Abdeen, MSc, PMP

Ahmad Khairiri Abdul Ghani, FIMechE, CEng

Habeeb Abdulla, MS, PMP

Jose Rafael Alcala Gomez, PMP

Emad A. Alghamdi, EMBA, PMP

Abdulaziz Hamed Alotaibi, PMP

Mohammad Alsalih

Abdulrahman Alulaiyan, MBA, PMP

Nahlah Alyamani, PMI-ACP, PgMP

Angelo Amaral, PMI-ACP, PMP

O. Arivazhagan "Ari", BE (Honours), PMP

Sivaram Athmakuri, PMI-ACP, PMP

Shahin Avak, BSc
Nabeel Eltyeb Babiker, P3O, PMP
Ammar N. Baidas, PgMP, PfMP
Herman Ballard
Bahadir V. Barbarosoglu, PhD, PMP
Eduardo Bazo Safra, MS, PMP
Gregory M. Becker, PMP
Nigel Blampied, PhD
Greta Blash, PMI-PBA, PgMP
Alessandro Calonico, PMP
Mario Coquillat, PMI-RMP, PMP
Gaurav Dhooper, SAFe4 Agilist, PMI-ACP
John D. Driessnack, CSM, PfMP
Nedal Dudin, PMI-ACP, PMP
Christopher L. Edwards, MBA, PMP
Mohamed R. Elkafoury, PhD, PMP
Michael J. Frenette, SMC, PMP
Juan Gantiva Vergara
Hisham Sami Ghulam, MBA, PMP
Theofanis Giotis, PhDc, PMP
Ivan Graff, PE, PMP
Simon J. Harris IPMO-E, PMP
Akram Hassan, PhD, PMP
Sergio Herrera-Apestigue, P3O, PMP
Dmitrii Ilenkov, PMP
David Kester
Suhail Khaled, PMI-ACP, PMP
Rouzbeh Kotobzadeh, PMP, PfMP
Boon Soon Lam
Kathleen E. Lane, EVP, PMP
Olivier Lazar
Derek D. Lehman

Zheng Lou
Medhat Mahmoud
Venkatram Vasi Mohanvasi
José S. Morales Brunet, MBA, PMP
Mordaka Maciej, PMI-ACP, PMP
Felipe Fernandes Moreira, PMP
Syed Ahsan Mustaqeem PE, PMP
Feras Nakeshbandy, PMI-RMP, PMP
Adriano Neves, PhD, PMP
Habeeb Omar, PgMP, PfMP
Truc Pham, PMI-ACP, PMP
Crispin ("Kik") Piney, PMP, PgMP
P. Ravikumar, PMP, PgMP
Gilberto Regal
Raman Rezaei
Juan Carlos Rincón Acuña, PhD, PMP
Bernard Roduit
Sachlani, PSM I, PMP
Abubaker Sami, PgMP, PfMP
Jovita Jayarama Shetty, CSM, PMP
Walla Siddig Elhadey, PMI-RMP, PMP
Islam Mohamed Soliman, PMP
Mauro Sotille
Laurent Thomas, PMI-ACP, PMP
Gaitan Marius Titi, PMI-PBA, PMP
Micol Trezza, MBA, PMP
Ali Vahedi Diz, PgMP, PfMP
Rajkumar Veera
Thierry Verlynde, MS, PMP
Dave Violette, MPM, PMP
Barb Waters, MBA, PMP
Michal P. Wieteska, ASEP, PMP

X2.3.3 PMI STANDARDS PROGRAM MEMBER ADVISORY GROUP (SMAG)

The PMI Standards Program Member Advisory Group (SMAG) works under the leadership of the standards manager. We extend out sincerest thanks to them for their compelling and helpful guidance throughout the development process.

During the course of the committee's work, the following distinguished members of the PMI community served with distinction on the SMAG:

Maria Cristina Barbero, CSM, PMI-ACP, PMP
Michael J. Frenette, I.S.P., SMC, MCITP, PMP
Brian Grafsgaard, CSM, PMP, PgMP, PfMP
David Gunner, MSc, PMP, PfMP
Hagit Landman, MBA, PMI-SP, PMP
Vanina Mangano, PMI-RMP, PMP
Yvan Petit, PhD, MEng, MBA, PMP, PfMP
Carolina Gabriela Spindola, MBA, SSBB, PMP

X2.3.4 CONSENSUS BODY REVIEW

The following individuals served as members of PMI Standards Program Consensus Body:

Nigel Blampied, PE, PMP
Chris Cartwright, MPM, PMP
John Dettbarn, DSc, PE
Charles Follin, PMP
Michael Frenette, PMP, SMC
Brian Grafsgaard, PMP, PgMP
Dave Gunner, PMP
Dorothy Kangas, MS, PMP
Thomas Kurihara
Hagit Landman, PMI-SP, PMP
Tim MacFadyen, MBA, PMP

Vanina Mangano, PMP
Mike Mosley, PE, PMP
Nanette Patton, MSBA, PMP
Crispin ("Kik") Piney, PgMP, PfMP
Mike Reed, PMP, PfMP
David Ross, PMP, PgMP
Paul Shaltry, PMP
C. Gabriela Spindola, CSSBB, PMP
Chris Stevens, PhD
Judi Vincent, BSc, BEd, PMP
David J. Violette, MPM, PMP

X2.3.5 HARMONIZATION TEAM CORE TEAM

Bridget Fleming, PMI-SP, PMP
Gregory Hart
Hagit Landman, PMI-SP, PMP
Timothy A. MacFadyen, MBA, PMP
Vanina Mangano, PMI-RMP, PMP
Mike Mosley
John Post, PMP
David W. Ross, PMP, PgMP
Cindy Shelton, PMI-ACP, PMP
Gary Sikma, PMI-ACP, PMP
Dave Violette, MPM, PMP

X2.3.6 PRODUCTION STAFF

Special mention is due to the following employees of PMI:

Kim Shinners, Product Coordinator
Roberta Storer, Product Specialist
Barbara Walsh, Product Manager, Publications

APPENDIX X3
APPLICATION OF EARNED VALUE MANAGEMENT (EVM) AT THE PORTFOLIO AND PROGRAM LEVELS

X3.1 EARNED VALUE MANAGEMENT (EVM) PRINCIPLES AT THE PORTFOLIO AND PROGRAM LEVELS

As noted in Section 1 of this standard, a principle-based philosophy underpins this standard. The intention is to incorporate the best earned value management (EVM) concepts and principles into high-level, results-oriented guidance without being too prescriptive with specific system implementation criteria. These concepts are best applied under a systems approach throughout the portfolio, program, and project management life cycles. An earned value management system (EVMS) deployment should also take into consideration the cultural acceptance of the system within the management framework of the organization in order to remain sustainable. A mature EVMS can be an important organizational process asset (OPA). Benefits from the application of the EVM methodology may increase when planned at a business unit level or above, before individual portfolio or program component baselines are set. As a portfolio, program, and project OPA, the business unit project management office (PMO) (or enterprise PMO [EPMO]) can maintain and tailor the methods to the performance management requirements per business unit or organization (e.g., a manual or an automated system and its incorporated tools, EVMS linkage to accounting and auditing processes, quality assurance framework, and quality controls). Such an approach best delivers the expected business value and ensures a continuing return on the investment applied to all organizational endeavors and change initiatives.

Earned value principles are applicable and quite useful for measuring performance at any management level (portfolio, program, and project). EVM principles may be used to reliably monitor the consumption of investments by measuring the consumption of allocated organizational resources. EVM may be used to monitor scope delivery at the specified quality by tracking completion rates, time variances, and so forth. In all cases and at any level (portfolio, program, or project), all measurements should be made from a predefined baseline. Naturally, baselines differ according to measurement parameters and objectives. For example, a portfolio accomplishment baseline may be used to report whether the whole portfolio is delivering its overall intended scope in time, to total portfolio budget and thus creating the envisioned value add for the organization. Practitioners may create performance indices that track actual progress results against the corresponding baseline at any given time during execution. For example:

◆ How many resources have been consumed given the overall work done?

◆ How much scope should have been accomplished given the time elapsed?

◆ How much time should have passed given the total work done?

When all levels are considered, EVM allows practitioners to manage time, cost, scope, benefits, economic added value, and return on investment. Instead of simply monitoring and reporting only qualitative performance results to key stakeholders, reliable quantitative results may be reported at all levels. Use of EVM above the project level often means organizations need to strengthen their benefits realization practices. This limitation is becoming more of an issue, as investments directed at specific portfolios and programs encompass more aspects of the organization as project-based work globally increases at steadfast rates. At the portfolio level, in order to maximize business value, practitioners should prioritize and reprioritize on a regular basis. Accomplished (earned) value concepts and principles may help to implement this requirement successfully. For example, EVM helps to reallocate resources when the cost is too high or the expected benefit is reduced for any reason.

At the portfolio and program levels, appropriate metrics (what we want to measure) and baselines should be developed. EVM has been primarily applied for measuring project-based work (scope, time, cost) under a predefined linear model (predetermined proportionality of cause-and-effect relationships leading to outputs/deliverables). This deterministic approach is applicable to a single portfolio or program component. Aggregates of all component metrics may be processed for portfolio or program performance reporting. Again, linearity is assumed or agreed and weighting factors are established for each component.

X3.2 APPLICATION OF EVM CONCEPTS FOR PERFORMANCE MANAGEMENT OF PORTFOLIOS AND PROGRAMS

Organizations need a way to clearly, quickly, and interactively identify, communicate, and measure benefits to know if they are on track to realize business value throughout an initiative. One of the significant challenges facing organizations that implement portfolio and program management is their capability to measure performance across the entire portfolio in a timely manner. Such information is vital to diagnose trends and identify portfolio or program components in need of prompt corrective action and improvement opportunities. Executives need validated information on overall portfolio trends, completion costs, and impacts on portfolio funding. Moreover, there is a need for increased up-to-date knowledge on the performance of the overall portfolio or program for quick decisions at both the management and governance domains. EVM principles (see Section 1.1) may prove valuable to analyze portfolio performance as EVM metrics may indicate not only how much money and effort were spent on a portfolio or program component, but also what *value* the organization generated for utilizing its resources. By using appropriate EVM concepts and principles, management can have reliable answers regarding the value generated by the organization from executing the whole portfolio with respect to committed and used organizational resources. Information obtained from EVM data can enable portfolio managers to take action to recover and improve performance in line with strategic objectives.

As briefly discussed in Section 1.4.1 of this standard, practitioners may apply EVM as a proven performance measurement method for portfolio and program components.

Note—The *Practice Standard for Earned Value Management* [11] did not provide any information on managing programs and portfolios. In Section G.14 of the practice standard, it was noted that EVM concepts may be applied to measure the performance of programs based on benefits realization and the performance of portfolios based on the creation of organizational values.

At the program and portfolio level, practitioners are able to apply three distinct approaches toward the implementation of an EVM system:

◆ Use of the standard EVM approaches for some or all program and project components. The same applies to portfolio components. Collect and aggregate earned value analysis component results for the whole portfolio or program. Weighing factors may be used related to each component's contribution to overall value-add at the portfolio level or benefits realization at the program level. At the portfolio level, such metrics may be particularly useful for the portfolio performance domains of strategic management, portfolio governance, and portfolio value management [5].

◆ At the program management level, since the program manager develops a program work breakdown structure (WBS), organizational breakdown structure (OBS), and a master schedule; all parts of the program management plan [12], and a benefits-based EVM methodology, similar to the methodology used for projects where benefits realization substitutes scope accomplishment. Overall program scope accomplishment is measured in terms of cost. Program management teams often use such an approach. This approach does not apply at the portfolio level.

Note—*The Standard for Program Management* [12] places EVM within the Program Life Cycle Management performance domain. The need for applying EVM is briefly described in Sections 7 and 8 of *The Standard for Program Management*.

◆ Managing a portfolio is about maximizing the delivery of value as defined by the strategic objectives of the organization or the business unit. Performance is based on organizational value-add, through the execution of portfolio components aligned continuously to organizational strategy. (Performance is based on the delivery of benefits at the program level and is based on the delivery of scope within the specified constraints at the project level.) In addition to aggregating earned value metrics for each portfolio component and developing performance results for the whole portfolio, portfolio practitioners may decide to create value realization metrics for the portfolio system as a whole. Under this approach, the metric is changed. At the portfolio level, it becomes benefits-dependent business value (or business result). EVM can still be run at the project and/or program level, focused on cost and benefits, while the portfolio level measures business value. Initially, benefits and corresponding interim benefits (also known as intermediate benefits or partial benefits) have to be clearly defined and mapped, often to the portfolio roadmap. (In the limited available literature for the application of earned value concepts at the portfolio and program levels, interim benefits are also known as intermediate benefits or partial benefits.) The portfolio roadmap can be expanded to include benefits depiction of the core phases of an organization's benefits life cycle across the project portfolio. Interim benefits need to be SMART and are usually monetized (SMART is an acronym for specific, measurable, achievable [or attainable], relevant, and time-bound). Apportionment techniques can be used to help capture related components and measure benefit. The same earned value (EV) principles and concepts described for projects in this standard are used to develop the performance measurement model.

The first and second approaches are based on the same EVM methodology. It should be noted that the first approach, namely the rolled-up, aggregated performance metrics obtainable from the application of EVM to each of the components, is the approach used most often for performance management at the portfolio or program levels. Specifically, it is the time and cost forecasting information obtained from the application of EVM to each of the components. This information is used for controlling overall resource support—not only cash flows, although cash flows are paramount. At the program level, the overall program cost in conjunction with the program master schedule is also used to determine an overall performance measurement baseline (PMB) for the whole program [12]. This PMB is used toward the monitoring and control of organizational resources. This is an important management function in all organizations. Senior management and portfolio governance need to have accurate information on overall resource utilization and particularly on how much each portfolio or program component will cost, and when each lump of funds will be required.

The third approach, introduced above, is a different method for practitioners to consider. It uses a roadmap of components for the whole portfolio or program, covering the delivery of all component outputs, which allows for the gradually accumulated benefit and consequently, to value-add at the portfolio level. Here the metric changes from overall scope to benefit over a set period of time. Such analysis requires a selection of a benefits period(s) that are mapped into the portfolio roadmap with identification on a component/interim benefits matrix (see note) [13]. Both need to be developed and incorporated into the portfolio strategic planning by the management team and agreed upon by all principal stakeholders. The development of a SMART model linking component deliverables to interim benefits is key. The modeled progress of the whole portfolio or program (i.e., the interim benefits realization that are associated with each component's progress) is considered to be roughly linear, timewise. For such an approach to be realistic, the whole system needs to be carefully analyzed, usually using visuals (e.g., sense-making models, tree maps, activity and information flow diagrams), so that component and subcomponent interdependencies are understood and accounted for. It should be noted that partial delivery of outputs does not coincide in time to program partial outcomes corresponding to interim benefits—often benefits come later. Awareness and understanding of such relations, unique for each portfolio or program, are critical for practical, meaningful implementation of earned value concepts.

Note—Benefits realization management (BRM) is the collective set of processes and practices for identifying benefits, measuring and evaluating benefits, and evaluating as well as aligning them with formal strategy. BRM ensures that benefits are realized as each project execution progresses and finishes, and that the benefits obtained are sustainable—and sustained—after each project implementation is complete.

At both levels, the application of earned value concepts for measuring performance and predicting future performance is required for setting a SMART benefits management baseline. For such a baseline, the benefit (instead of the cost), given the scope within the roadmap, is the measured variable over time. Once a SMART benefits management baseline is developed, based on the portfolio roadmap and the components' outputs/benefits matrix, reliable methods for measurements from this time-phased baseline are tested and established. Once a realistic model has been created, variances between planned and/or envisioned benefits and achieved, earned benefits at any given time within the portfolio/program life cycle may be calculated.

This approach entails systems thinking and involves treating the whole portfolio or program as a system. In practice, most portfolios and programs fall under this category. Using earned value concepts, portfolio practitioners may measure the benefit creation process (or the business value creation process) in a time-phased manner, to be able to answer the question "how am I doing toward achieving the specific business or strategic benefit" using both current measurements and estimates at completion. To create such a baseline, practitioners should take a deterministic approach (assume a rough linearity), assume causality (proportional cause/effect relationships), assume minimal effects due to the portfolio system component and subcomponent interdependencies, and assume a state of reduced complexity (e.g., minimal emergence of unknown risks, issues, problems).

Awareness of the presence of complexity and how it may affect performance plus vigilance toward a realistic situational model, adapted to current conditions, at all times, should always be present. Practitioners should be cautious when trying to apply linear thinking-based measurement methods to nonlinear phenomena always present in the complex parts of system(s). On the other hand, the advantage of being able to examine a program or a portfolio in detail (relationship-wise) under proven successful practices of earned value management may result in a thorough understanding of the real functioning of the whole program or portfolio system.

As briefly mentioned previously, a SMART benefits management baseline is key. A recommended approach toward creating such a benefits management baseline is first to develop a benefits-informed portfolio strategic plan, roadmap, and performance measures for the whole portfolio or program (interim benefits linked to component outputs), and to create a component-benefits matrix. Organizations have recommended the creation of critical questions regarding portfolio value to assist in guiding value modeling. Other approaches entail a logical dependency network of key system components that can be read in both directions. The roadmap links each component to the corresponding interim benefit(s). It is necessary to contain essential model information in each node of the visual representation of the system, so that progress can be measured and estimates to completion of the roadmap can be visualized. Consideration should be given to the fact that some program components produce immediate benefits, while others require beforehand transition activities. It is paramount that measurements are consistent and depict accurate, real situational conditions; otherwise, efficient controls will not be attainable. Erroneous measurements usually lead to wrong managerial decisions.

A benefits realization management (BRM) framework has to be established for the portfolio or the program [14]. Once the benefits map is developed and agreed upon, a time-phased benefits realization roadmap may be created. This roadmap is used for the establishment of the benefits PMB. The objective is to measure variances from the benefits management baseline reliably, so the model may provide answers to practitioners regarding what interim benefits were planned to be achieved and how many have been delivered.

Using this approach, issues to address and manage include the plethora of nondeterministic component elements and their attributes, particularly at the portfolio level. At the portfolio level, this approach may considerably influence the creation of a SMART measurement baseline based on planned and earned value-add. The intangible parts of both value-add and interim benefits are another concern. Emergent situations and risks from component interrelationships requiring adaptability toward realistic and measurable interim benefits versus envisioned interim benefits, influenced by human behavioral factors, is a further cause of enhanced complexity.

The mapped interim benefits may be used to measure progress, since smaller chunks may be more realistically modeled with linear models. Interim benefits should be linked to portfolio and/or program components and these to subcomponents; subsequent control accounts may then be created. In essence, EVM is a rational, deterministic methodology. Benefits maps should include realistic many-to-one relationships between the work packages, the control accounts, and every single portfolio (or program) component or subcomponent. The accuracy in modeling these relationships (including their feedback loops) is very important toward defining meaningful interim benefits, particularly at the portfolio level. Realistic positioning of each interim benefit and consequential value-add within the integrated timescale of the portfolio is critical for meaningful measurements and management of overall performance at these levels.

Portfolio performance information should also include information about each component's progress, which component outputs have been delivered (also at what point in the portfolio life cycle), and what component outputs or deliverables add value to the organization in the specified timeframe. The concept is to apply what the practitioner does at the project level for control accounts to portfolio components (if necessary, for some components at the subcomponent level), and create corresponding control accounts. Practitioners may take a design thinking approach by developing performance measurement solutions in line with both the business case and customer/owner experience and expectations. Successful implementation of such EV concepts may provide justification for creating a benefit-focused culture to quantify and calculate the need for a long-term view. Portfolio governance, which reviews the business cases for all strategic initiatives, will need to discuss and approve the identified benefits and proposed measurement methods. Governance needs to be convinced that this approach goes beyond budget, scope, and schedule. It is primarily about reporting and visually communicating business impact.

For the development and integration of component interim benefit estimates, practitioners do not need to make detailed estimates at the beginning. On the other hand, practitioners should have an overall estimate for the whole portfolio or program. Rolling wave estimation of interim benefits may prove adequate. Available literature indicates that the whole process is not only about fairly accurate forecasting—it is also about awareness, about the management team's understanding of the strategic purpose, system structure, and envisioned and planned outcomes or benefits of the whole portfolio or program.

APPENDIX X4
PERFORMANCE MANAGEMENT EXAMPLE

X4.1 IMPLEMENTING EARNED VALUE MANAGEMENT TO MANAGE PERFORMANCE DURING THE DESIGN AND CONSTRUCTION OF A SMART BUILDING

The purpose of this appendix is to provide an example that shows how a project team can manage execution and performance using earned value management (EVM). The example is an internal project for an organization with some activity contracted to a vendor, but EVM requirements are not flowed down to the vendors. This example incorporates a variety of techniques for illustrative purposes to help the reader imagine real-world situations and possibilities available for use by a project team.

In this example, some project activities are going to fall under the EVM baseline, while others will be managed outside of the baseline. Control accounts (CA) CA-001 through CA-004 are within the baseline, while CA-005 (Smart Building Handover Phase) is managed outside of the baseline. This is a choice made by the owner of the organization, who, in this example, is executing a project similar to other projects the organization has executed in the past. Examination and incorporation of lessons learned from prior projects indicates that the activities in CA-005 have a high probability of success. Managing this CA external to the EVM baseline enables the project controls manager to finalize the performance management activities as the project closes. The leadership could have chosen to apply EVM to only the contracted portion of the effort. However, their previous experience indicated there was value added to implement EVM across internal efforts. The net result is that the team uses EVM where it provides value in assisting the team in managing project delivery.

This example uses an experienced organization with an internal project team executing a relatively standard turnkey project for engineering and construction. Purposely, the example was kept generic and at a fairly high level. The example assumes an experienced team that has built several smart buildings for the organization. This is a fairly simple example, thus all management details, technical details, and implementation conditions that come about in real-life conditions have been omitted to keep the example short.

The example shows the flow and interdependence of the fundamental practices of EVM as they are outlined in this standard. This is summarized in the following list:

◆ Establish a project charter and make basic decisions on how EVM will be used (see Section 2).

◆ Plan the project with EVM (see Sections 3.1 and 3.2).

◆ Establish project baselines and the integrated performance measurement baseline (PMB) (see Sections 3.3–3.5).

   ■ Decompose scope by developing the work breakdown structure (WBS) and establish the team structure with an organizational breakdown structure (OBS).

   ■ Develop a CA plan using a responsibility assignment matrix (RAM).

   ■ Assign clear accountability and responsibility for each CA.

   ■ Develop a time-phased budget for each CA, using work and planning packages.

      ○ In this example, a resource-loaded schedule was developed and used. Therefore, a time-phased budget with a breakdown to the activity level should be made available.

      ○ This example has an initial, detailed plan for one CA, with the other CAs reflected in planning packages. All the CAs are further planned in detailed work packages prior to initiating the work and are consistent with the evolution of the project.

   ■ Assign an earned value (EV) measurement technique to each work package (WP).

      ○ Purposefully, a variety of objective measurement techniques are used to illustrate the diversity of measurement methods.

   ■ Baseline the PMB.

      ○ A resource-loaded schedule is used that identifies the EV measurement techniques in the schedule. This allows for baselining the PMB and the total project in the scheduling tool.

   ■ Maintain the integrity of PMB throughout project execution with formal change control procedures by using the baseline capability in the example's schedule tool.

◆ Measure and analyze performance against the baseline (see Section 4).

   ■ Record resource consumption during project execution.

   ■ Measure the physical work progress objectively using the EV measurement techniques previously chosen.

   ■ Derive EV.

   ■ Analyze and forecast cost and schedule performance.

   ■ Report performance.

   ■ Identify and implement management actions as appropriate.

X4.2 INITIATING A PROJECT WITH EVM (SEE SECTION 2)

During project initiation, the project charter is issued and the project stakeholders are identified. Development of the project charter should include:

◆ Overall approach to implement the EVM system,

◆ Management requirements for implementation of the EVMS, and

◆ Expected benefits from using EVM.

The following is a basic charter outline for this example project.

X4.2.1 PROJECT TITLE

The project title for this example is "Design and Construction of a Smart Building."

X4.2.2 PROJECT DESCRIPTION

The project is to deliver the engineering design, procurement, and construction of a smart building on property that has already been acquired. This project includes the information technology (IT) design, applications software development, hardware procurement and installation work of the smart features of the building, and the commissioning/handover activities.

Note—The description presented is purposely not detailed and simplified to allow singular focus on the use of EVM. This example may be tailored by practitioners and can be used for any other types of projects, as well as for training purposes. A robust description of the project and the product(s) would be included in this section of the project charter. The description would include the boundaries of the project or any specific elements, and items that the project scope should exclude.

X4.2.3 PROJECT PURPOSE AND JUSTIFICATION

The purpose of this project is the turnkey delivery of a smart building from conception through engineering design, construction, development, and installation of an integrated smart building system having an Internet of Things (IoT) platform and gateways, and finishing with commissioning/handover.

Note—The Internet of Things (IoT) is an emergent term that refers to a network of equipment, sensors, and other products that are interconnected and identifiable throught the building's digital network via the internet.

The smart building should meet all technical specifications in addition to the project performance parameters within the cost and schedule requirements as established by the project stakeholders. A summary of information from the business case of the project could be included in this section as well as the envisioned, expected benefits.

X4.2.4 MEASURABLE PROJECT OBJECTIVES AND RELATED SUCCESS CRITERIA

The project objective is the delivery of the smart building in accordance with project requirements provided by the owner as inputs.

The project success criteria are the completion on time and on budget to the owner's provided requirements, meeting project scope and quality specifications.

X4.2.5 HIGH-LEVEL REQUIREMENTS

The project implements and uses the organization's earned value management system (EVMS) for the management of its performance. The management team decided that the handover phase (CA-005) will be managed outside of the EVM baseline (PMB), thus allowing the project team to close down monitoring and control processes as the handover efforts are completed. This decision is based on experience and a risk assessment. The project team uses EVM to manage the various CAs, some of which use outside vendors. Additional technical high-level requirements should be defined in this section of the project charter.

Note—In this example, it is assumed that the project team is experienced and that well-defined organizational process assets (OPAs)/enterprise environmental factors (EEFs) exist in the organization for the various Knowledge Areas within the *PMBOK® Guide*. This example demonstrates the concept that EVM doesn't need to be applied in an all-or-nothing scenario, but should be applied based on management needs, especially relative to project risks.

X4.2.5.1 PROJECT RISK

The Building Construction control account (CA-003) has a contingency reserve (CR) of $50,000 based on the organization's prior experiences with risk management within this CA. These include weather, site clearing, and material price fluctuation. The overall project has a management reserve (MR) established based on prior project experiences and remaining budget.

Note—If the organization implementing the project has a method to characterize the overall risk of this project based on historical information from past projects, it should be defined here. For this example, the team has extensive experience working together and on the construction of smart buildings, thus a CR and MR that are less than 10% of the project budget was adopted.

X4.2.5.2 SUMMARY MILESTONE SCHEDULE

The project is scheduled to start and complete within 15 months. The planning is completed within 7 months after the design is completed, with civil work completed within 13 months.

Note—This section should define high-level milestones for the project, deadlines, schedule constraints, and any identified major dependencies, external or internal.

X4.2.5.3 BUDGET AND PREAPPROVED FINANCIAL RESOURCES

The project estimate is $1,500,000:

◆ Initial funding authorization is $500,000 (pending completion of detailed planning).

◆ Contingency and management reserves will be less than 10% of the project estimate. (This is a tradition within the company, as they generally do not do very risky projects.)

X4.2.5.4 KEY STAKEHOLDERS LIST

Define roles of stakeholders, if any:

◆ Organization's PMO;

◆ Organization's leadership: owner/president, chief financial officer, and chief information officer;

◆ Organization's property management group (internal customer);

◆ Architectural/engineering/building firms; and

◆ Agile software firm.

X4.2.5.5 PROJECT APPROVAL REQUIREMENTS

Project approval requirements cover: (a) what constitutes project success, (b) who decides that the project is successful, and (c) who approves the project.

◆ **Project exit criteria.** This requirement covers what conditions are to be met in order to close or cancel the project or phase. In this case, it is the end state at turnover.

◆ **Assigned project manager.** The project management office (PMO) should assign the project manager with noted responsibility and authority level.

◆ **Project sponsor.** In this example, the property management group director is the project sponsor.

X4.3 PLANNING A PROJECT USING EVM

During the project planning process, the *PMBOK® Guide* calls for scope, schedule, and cost baselines to be set. When using EVM, those baselines are integrated into a PMB (see Section 3). Implementation of EVM amplifies the importance of integrating the project planning, especially the processes that create quantitative baselines related to scope, schedule, and cost, considering resources and risk management.

In this example, we are considering the design and construction of a smart building, which includes the design and construction of the building including civil and mechanical components, as well as a smart building approach that integrates appliances onto a single information technology backplane that will serve as a centralized interface to an integrated monitoring and control system for the building. The goal is to provide a capability that the building customers can use that provides sufficient intelligence to the building and integrates systems to maximize the use of renewable energy sources, ensure safety and security, and enable the integration of compatible and intelligent customer appliances installed in the building.

In this example, the project team has developed plans as an integrated project management plan that addresses each Knowledge Area. The team has addressed the organization's EEFs and OPAs and made all the appropriate decisions needed for planning in an EVM context. The team in this example has used EVM before and built an integrated project management plan; therefore, based on their experience, further process and procedural development is not needed. See Section 3, Section 3.1–2 for details to consider.

The culmination of the scope planning processes is to develop a WBS as the single structure that integrates the scope, schedule, and cost baselines. The team establishes the OBS and integrates it with the WBS to define the RAM. The RAM for this example is shown in Figure X4-1.

Performance Management Example

WBS	Title
01	Smart Building Project
1.1	Project Management
1.2	Planning
1.3	Smart Building
1.3.1	Building
1.3.2	Information System
1.4	Handover

#	Control Account	WBS	OBS	Budget
CA-001	Project Management	1.1	01.01	$336,000
CA-002	Planning Phase	1.2	01.02	$67,700
CA-003	Construction	1.3.1	01.03	$928,080
CA-004	Information System	1.3.2	01.04	$61,280
			PMB	$1,393,060
CA-005	Handover Phase	1.4	01.01	$13,700
			Management Reserve	$93,240
			Project Budget	$1,500,000

OBS	Title
01	Project Team
01.01	Controls Team
01.02	Design Team
01.03	Construction Team
01.04	Scrum Team

Figure X4-1. Example of Responsibility Assignment Matrix (RAM) for Smart Building

For this example, the project organizational structure is broken down to the team level. The teams gathered various members from the organization's internal groups, such as engineering, procurement, construction, and software to form a matrix organization for the project. The matrix organization also folds in vendor/contractor personnel. The project controls team is internal, from the PMO. The bulk of the engineering and construction work is executed by contractors, who are a part of the design and construction teams. The organization also uses a very experienced team to build the smart building application and underlying information management system, which will pull the IoT components of the building and customer appliances together.

The team derived five CAs, which define key intersection points within the RAM. This enables delegation of responsibility and identification of accountability for project management and performance to an appropriate level. This is a decision made by the project management team for the purpose of managing the project. The construction CA (CA-003), with a budget that is almost two-thirds of the project, could have been broken down with a separate CA for each of the WPs. In this case, it is not necessary, and would only add to the overhead and provide little value.

Note—The CAs are at different levels of the WBS, with CA-001, CA-002, and CA-005 at one level of the WBS, while CA-003 and CA-004 are at the next, lower level of the WBS.

During planning, the team determines the planned use of contingency and management reserves. For this project, the team is going to follow the *PMBOK® Guide* breakout of these reserves, which were outlined in the charter during the initiation phase. The team has decided to spread the CR over a period of time within the building construction CA, consistent with the temporal risk assessment.[3] This helps the team understand the potential funding profile needs. Alternative approaches include profiling the CR at the beginning or end of the CA activities or holding the CR at the project level in some fashion. Planning should also define who within the project team is authorized to use contingency reserve. For instance, although the CR is applied to CAs to more robustly assign where the risk response budget is assigned, project processes may still require the project manager's authorization for its use or enable the CA manager to access the budget.

With the RAM established, the team now develops and integrates plan activities and resources within the project schedule (see Section X4.4). The full scope of work for each WP should be scheduled and resourced (see Table X4-1). The example starts within the first CA (CA-001) in the first work package, WP-01 (Project Management). The level of effort (LOE) EV technique is used. After the initial planning is complete, one can switch to an apportionment approach in WP-02 (Manage Product Realization). This would then apportion the value earned to the other CAs/WPs in the baseline. In the case of this simplified example, this would complicate the performance data processing. Since the example is not using an earned value commercial tool, the example continues with LOE as the EV technique. Next, the detailed planning of CA-001 and CA-002 is completed, with three work packages each (WP-01, WP-02, WP-03, and then WP-04, WP-05, and WP-06). The other CAs (CA-003, CA-004, and CA-005) contain only planning packages at this point in time. These CAs and the associated planning packages will be detailed as part of CA-002, WP-04, WP-05, and WP-06 as the design matures. The project controls team assists the managers of the control accounts with this planning as part of their work in WP-02. This approach uses the rolling wave concept (see Section 6.2.2.3 of the *PMBOK® Guide* and Section 3.4.1.3 of this standard).

From this point forward, it is assumed that the total project has been planned in detail and converted to work packages using the rolling wave approach. The cost breakdown is provided in Table X4-1. This table shows the cost estimate developed for the project using a bottom-up approach based on the resource-loaded schedule and schedule-driven quantities. The project team established contracts with various vendors with set labor rates and/or unit prices. The project requirements and the architectural/engineering design are of sufficient maturity to enable high confidence in both durations and the fixed-price efforts for design and construction. The IT development and implementation team decided to use an agile approach, namely Scrum. The agile Scrum team, which is building the smart building information system application, is on the company's long-standing time and material contract and is priced with labor hours. A risk-based contingency reserve was also established for CA-003 to bring the overall project plan to a level of confidence acceptable to the organization. See Section X4.4 for further discussion of how the CR package is handled.

---

[3] For completeness in illustrating the example thought process, a line (CR-01) has been included in Figure X4-2. This line is intended to show the relationship of the risk reserve to the plan elements with which it is associated, both in terms of the associated timeframe and resources. There is no intent to portray this line as an element of the WBS or logically link it as an activity in the schedule.

Table X4-1. Resource Table

Resource Name	Work	Cost	Material Label	Standard Rate
Project Manager	568 hrs	$56,800.00		$100.00/hr
Project Controls Manager	568 hrs	$45,440.00		$80.00/hr
Scheduler	264 hrs	$15,840.00		$60.00/hr
Risk Analyst	264 hrs	$15,840.00		$60.00/hr
Cost Estimator	264 hrs	$15,840.00		$60.00/hr
EVM Specialist	264 hrs	$15,840.00		$60.00/hr
Procurement Manager	164 hrs	$13,120.00		$80.00/hr
Engineering Manager	608 hrs	$48,640.00		$80.00/hr
Civil Specialist	144 hrs	$8,640.00		$60.00/hr
Electrical Specialist	128 hrs	$7,680.00		$60.00/hr
Mechanical Specialist	112 hrs	$6,720.00		$60.00/hr
IT Specialist	96 hrs	$5,760.00		$60.00/hr
Construction Manager	780 hrs	$62,400.00		$80.00/hr
Quality Assurance	112 hrs	$6,720.00		$60.00/hr
Logistics Manager	96 hrs	$5,760.00		$60.00/hr
HR Manager	548 hrs	$32,880.00		$60.00/hr
Quantity Surveyor	288 hrs	$17,280.00		$60.00/hr
Supervision Engineers	444 hrs	$26,640.00		$60.00/hr
Application Manager	624 hrs	$49,920.00		$80.00/hr
Agile Developer #1	498 hrs	$39,840.00		$80.00/hr
Agile Developer #2	488 hrs	$34,160.00		$70.00/hr
Engineering Design	1 FP	$25,000.00	FP	$25,000.00
Logistical Transport Services	1,000 kg-km	$20,000.00	kg-km	$20.00
Building Construction	1 FP	$550,000.00	FP	$550,000.00
Interior and Decoration	$100,000	$100,000.00	$	$1,000.00
Gardening Services	$60,000	$60,000.00	$	$1,000.00
IT Infrastrucrure	1 FP	$65,000.00	FP	$65,000.00
System Specialist Consultant	50 Person-Hour	$5,000.00	Person-Hour	$100.00
Building Risk Contingency Reserve	$50,000	$50,000.00	$	$1.00
	TOTAL	**$1,406,760.00**		

X4.4 EXECUTING AND MONITORING AND CONTROLLING A PROJECT USING EVM

As noted in Section 3, the example project starts off within the first CA (CA-001) in the first WP, Project Management (WP-01). All other resources are in planning packages in CA-001 and the other CAs. The example uses rolling wave planning and then details are planned for the rest of CA-001 and CA-002, followed by detail planning for CA-003 to CA-005 during the project planning phase that occurs within CA-002.

Although no detailed planning has been accomplished beyond CA-001 and WP-01, project work starts with CA-001/WP-01 and the project moves into the use of executing and monitoring and controlling processes. The objective is to execute the plan, accomplish work, collect data, produce EVM metrics, analyze performance, and make decisions. See Section 4 for more details. One consideration might be to add schedule activities to plan the remaining CAs and WPs, except for the agile portion of the project where the Scrum agile approach employs sprints to iteratively establish work to be accomplished.

In the project executing process, EVM requires the measurement of performance and recording of resource consumption and associated cost, usually in monetary value.

Note—EVM strives to objectively measure the physical progress of work. The more this technique achieves this goal, the better it performs its role of performance management, and the more it contributes to effective project management. Projects vary a lot in regard to the physical qualities of their work. For example, most construction projects consist largely of tangible products, which can be readily and directly measured. Many research projects, however, yield only intangible outcomes until their final product emerges at the end. Although objective measures of physical progress are preferred, some measure of work scope accomplishment, including a subjective assessment of progress, is better than none at all.

For an analysis of the whole process, refer to Section 4 of this standard. Note that measurement, whether performance or actual cost (AC), needs to be captured in such a way that permits their comparison with the PMB. Therefore, work progress is measured in the manner in which it was planned to be measured, based on the EV technique in the PMB. Using these measured earned value (EV) data, the planned value (PV) data from the PMB, and the measured actual data (usually, this is cost data, but it could be hours or another measure), the project controls team calculates basic EVM metrics at the work package level and rolls the information up to the CA or entire project level and reports EVM results as needed. Usually, PV, EV, and AC are collected at the same level, the WP level, but this is not necessary. AC could be collected at an aggregate CA level while PV and EV are at the WP level. In the example, planning and measuring are at the same level. Only within WP-14 and WP-15 has measuring EV with milestones at the activity level occurred below the WP level. See Section 4.4 for further information on EV metrics.

After significant decisions have been made in the planning phase of the project, the team completes the detail planning of all CAs and WPs. Figure X4-2 represents that schedule. With the scope further planned and understood in detail, the schedule detailed, and the resources estimated and allocated to schedule activities, the team followed the appropriate change control for CA-003, CA-004, and CA-005 to update the time-phased project baseline (total project) and the PMB set with CA-001 to CA-004.

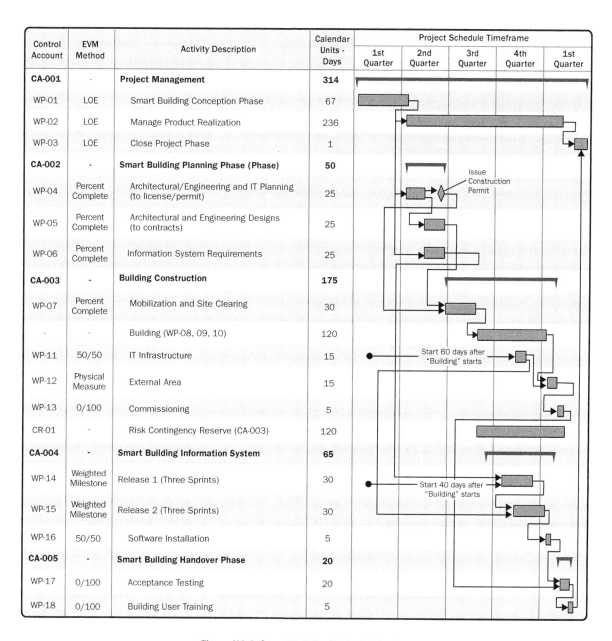

Control Account	EVM Method	Activity Description	Calendar Units - Days	Project Schedule Timeframe				
				1st Quarter	2nd Quarter	3rd Quarter	4th Quarter	1st Quarter
CA-001	-	**Project Management**	**314**					
WP-01	LOE	Smart Building Conception Phase	67					
WP-02	LOE	Manage Product Realization	236					
WP-03	LOE	Close Project Phase	1					
CA-002	-	**Smart Building Planning Phase (Phase)**	**50**					
WP-04	Percent Complete	Architectural/Engineering and IT Planning (to license/permit)	25					
WP-05	Percent Complete	Architectural and Engineering Designs (to contracts)	25					
WP-06	Percent Complete	Information System Requirements	25					
CA-003	-	**Building Construction**	**175**					
WP-07	Percent Complete	Mobilization and Site Clearing	30					
-	-	Building (WP-08, 09, 10)	120					
WP-11	50/50	IT Infrastructure	15					
WP-12	Physical Measure	External Area	15					
WP-13	0/100	Commissioning	5					
CR-01	-	Risk Contingency Reserve (CA-003)	120					
CA-004	-	**Smart Building Information System**	**65**					
WP-14	Weighted Milestone	Release 1 (Three Sprints)	30					
WP-15	Weighted Milestone	Release 2 (Three Sprints)	30					
WP-16	50/50	Software Installation	5					
CA-005	-	**Smart Building Handover Phase**	**20**					
WP-17	0/100	Acceptance Testing	20					
WP-18	0/100	Building User Training	5					

Figure X4-2. Smart Building Project Schedule

Table X4-1 shows the resource name/type, the quantities, and the total cost of resources that are estimated to be consumed in each work package.

Note—The allocation is based on which work will consume the resources (economic perspective), rather than when the resources are eventually acquired and paid for (cash-flow perspective).

The project manager, in accordance with the organization's OPA, authorizes the work packages as they are opened and work is started under the baseline. Initially the project manager authorizes WP-01 and then WP-02 through WP-06. After all the detailed planning is completed, the other WPs are authorized.

Data are collected (see Section 4.3) using simple spreadsheets that collect the status of scope, schedule, and cost on a weekly basis. The project/program control teams send out a status sheet on Thursday afternoon to each manager of the open CAs and get responses back from the team by Monday midmorning. The schedule and other status sheets are updated before the late afternoon team meeting on Monday. If any of the data required are not known, the manager of the CAs provides an estimated actual. The sheets also provide a place for managers to note any concerns or state if any part of their plan needs to be changed.

The program control team calculates performance metrics (see Section 4.4), which are provided to each CA manager during the weekly Monday afternoon team meeting. Sections X4.4.1 through X4.4.5 provide snapshots of various time periods, discussions within the team, and the management actions taken.

X4.4.1 WEEK 10 (YEAR 1)

In WP-01 (Smart Building Conception Phase), the team is running 5% over budget in actuals, but is estimating that CA-002 and WP-04 (Architectural/Engineering and IT Planning) will start on time in a couple weeks with the engineering integrated product team (IPT) (see Table X4-2). Management IPT realizes that the scheduler is new and has been taking a little more time than the PMO's more experienced schedulers. The team decides this is not a concern. The weather prediction for the summer and fall are looking better than normal, so this is an opportunity for the overall project to come in considerably under budget.

Table X4-2. EVM Data at 10 Weeks—Smart Building Conception Phase

CA	BAC	PV	AC	EV	CV	CPI	SV	SPI	EAC_{cpi}	$TCPI_{bac}$	VAC
CA-001	**$336,000**	**$13,325**	**$13,992**	**$13,325**	**($666)**	**0.95**	**$0**	**1.00**	**$352,800**	**1.00**	**($16,800)**
WP-01	$19,840	$13,325	$13,992	$13,325	($666)	0.95	$0	1.00	$20,832	1.00	($992)
WP-02	$267,600								$267,600	1.00	$0
WP-03	$18,560								$18,560	1.00	$0
CA-002	**$67,700**								**$67,700**	**1.00**	**$0**
WP-04	$24,100								$24,100	1.00	$0
WP-05	$24,100								$24,100	1.00	$0
WP-06	$19,500								$19,500	1.00	$0
CA-003	**$928,080**								**$928,080**	**1.00**	**$0**
CR-01	$50,000								$50,000	1.00	$0
WP-07	$31,380								$31,380	1.00	$0
WP-08	$380,760								$380,760	1.00	$0
WP-09	$98,540								$98,540	1.00	$0
WP-10	$119,080								$119,080	1.00	$0
WP-11	$71,680								$71,680	1.00	$0
WP-12	$173,600								$173,600	1.00	$0
WP-13	$3,040								$3,040	1.00	$0
CA-004	**$61,280**								**$61,280**	**1.00**	**$0**
WP-14	$30,260								$30,260	1.00	$0
WP-15	$29,760								$29,760	1.00	$0
WP-16	$1,260								$1,260	1.00	$0
CA-005	**$13,700**								**$13,700**	**1.00**	**$0**
WP-17	$11,540								$11,540	1.00	$0
WP-18	$2,160								$2,160	1.00	$0
TOTAL	**$1,406,760**	**$13,325**	**$13,992**	**$13,325**	**($666)**	**0.95**	**$0**	**1.00**	**$1,477,098**	**1.00**	**($70,338)**

X4.4.2 WEEK 25 (YEAR 1)

CA-002 (Smart Building Planning Phase) has completed WP-04 and WP-05 on time and 29% under budget (see Table X4-3). Most members of the team were tasked with other efforts within the organization and were very efficient in completing their work during the past few months. The engineering design vendor stayed on schedule and no changes were needed to affect the fixed-price contract. However, WP-06 (Information System Requirements) is running behind by a few weeks because team members were unable to be more efficient with their dual tasking, but plan to come within budget. The team was able to complete all aspects that affected the civil works (WP-08), so the 2-week delay only affects WP-09, which doesn't start for several months. Therefore, the team determines there is no impact to the project. At this point, the team decides to push back the CR package, which was time phased to start in week 31. The team pushed the package back to week 45, the start of WP-11 (IT Infrastructure).

Table X4-3. EVM Data at 25 Weeks (Year 1)—Smart Building Planning Phase

CA	BAC	PV	AC	EV	CV	CPI	SV	SPI	EAC_{cpi}	$TCPI_{bac}$	VAC
CA-001	$336,000	$86,674	$91,008	$86,674	($4,334)	0.95	$0	1.00	$352,800	1.02	($16,800)
WP-01	$19,840	$19,840	$20,832	$19,840	($992)	0.95	$0	1.00	$20,832	1.00	($992)
WP-02	$267,600	$66,834	$70,176	$66,834	($3,342)	0.95	$0	1.00	$312,480	1.01	$14,880
WP-03	$18,560								$18,560	1.00	$0
CA-002	$67,700	$67,700	$49,728	$64,268	$14,540	1.29	($3,432)	0.95	$52,384	0.19	$15,316
WP-04	$24,100	$24,100	$17,111	$24,100	$6,989	1.41	$0	1.00	$17,111	0.00	$6,989
WP-05	$24,100	$24,100	$17,111	$24,100	$6,989	1.41	$0	1.00	$17,111	0.00	$6,989
WP-06	$19,500	$19,500	$15,506	$16,068	$562	1.04	($3,432)	0.82	$8,818	0.86	$682
CA-003	$928,080	$3,138	$3,138	$3,138	$0	1.00	$0	1.00	$928,080	1.00	$0
CR-01	$50,000								$50,000	1.00	$0
WP-07	$31,380	$3,138	$3,138	$3,138	$0	1.00	$0	1.00	$31,380	1.00	$0
WP-08	$380,760								$380,760	1.00	$0
WP-09	$98,540								$98,540	1.00	$0
WP-10	$119,080								$119,080	1.00	$0
WP-11	$71,680								$71,680	1.00	$0
WP-12	$173,600								$173,600	1.00	$0
WP-13	$3,040								$3,040	1.00	$0
CA-004	$61,280								$61,280	1.00	$0
WP-14	$30,260								$30,260	1.00	$0
WP-15	$29,760								$29,760	1.00	$0
WP-16	$1,260								$1,260	1.00	$0
CA-005	$13,700								$13,700	1.00	$0
WP-17	$11,540								$11,540	1.00	$0
WP-18	$2,160								$2,160	1.00	$0
TOTAL	$1,406,760	$157,512	$143,874	$154,080	$10,206	1.07	($3,432)	1.00	$1,313,579	0.99	$93,181

X4.4.3 WEEK 44 (YEAR 1)

At this point, all the CAs in the PMB (CA-001, CA-002, CA-003, and CA-004) are open with numerous work packages (see Table X4-4 and Figure X4-3).

CA-003, especially WP-08 (Civil Works), has completed 3 weeks early, which the team was able to predict because they were tracking EV using the construction contractor's table of values as a physical measure of completed work. The work completed early from the start of the WP. This allowed the team to plan to start several other WPs early per the schedule network.

The Scrum team started CA-004 3 weeks early (week 40), which was possible because the team was able to predict early starts as they tracked not only the schedule, but also EV metrics during early portions of the building construction (CA-003) efforts.

The team also decides, given the positive weather forecast and good progress, to move the CR package budget to management reserve (MR). This adjusts the total PMB value down by $50,000 and increases the MR account by an equal amount. This move is performed under formal change control. At this point, the team also decides to adjust their estimate to complete (ETC) for both the cost and schedule. The project manager sends a report to the company leadership that the project is likely to come under budget by $100,000 ($1.5 million to $1.4 million) and complete up to 4 weeks early. See Section 4.5 for more information.

Table X4-4. EVM Data at 44 Weeks (Year 1)

CA	BAC	PV	AC	EV	CV	CPI	SV	SPI	EAC$_{cpi}$	TCPI$_{bac}$	VAC
CA-001	**$336,000**	**$206,470**	**$216,794**	**$206,470**	**($10,324)**	**0.95**	**$0**	**1.00**	**$352,800**	**1.09**	**($16,800)**
WP-01	$19,840	$19,840	$20,832	$19,840	($992)	0.95	$0	1.00	$20,832	0.00	($992)
WP-02	$267,600	$186,630	$195,962	$186,630	($9,332)	0.95	$0	1.00	$312,480	1.09	($14,880)
WP-03	$18,560								$18,560	1.00	$0
CA-002	**$67,700**	**$67,700**	**$54,057**	**$67,700**	**$13,643**	**1.25**	**$0**	**1.00**	**$54,057**	**0.00**	**$13,643**
WP-04	$24,100	$24,100	$17,111	$24,100	$6,989	1.41	$0	1.00	$17,111	0.00	$6,989
WP-05	$24,100	$24,100	$17,111	$24,100	$6,989	1.41	$0	1.00	$17,111	0.00	$6,989
WP-06	$19,500	$19,500	$19,835	$19,500	($335)	0.98	$0	1.00	$19,835	0.00	($335)
CA-003	**$878,080**	**$260,283**	**$324,785**	**$324,785**	**$0**	**1.00**	**$64,503**	**1.24**	**$878,080**	**1.00**	**$0**
CR-01	$0	$0					$0		$0	1.00	$0
WP-07	$31,380	$31,380	$31,380	$3,138	$0	1.00	$0	1.00	$31,380	1.00	$0
WP-08	$380,760	$215,764	$246,701	$246,701	$0	1.00	$30,937	1.14	$380,760	1.00	$0
WP-09	$98,540	$13,139	$37,774	$37,774	$0	1.00	$24,635	2.87	$98,540	1.00	$0
WP-10	$119,080		$8,931	$8,931	$0	1.00	$8,931	[A]	$119,080	1.00	$0
WP-11	$71,680								$71,680	1.00	$0
WP-12	$173,600								$173,600	1.00	$0
WP-13	$3,040								$3,040	1.00	$0
CA-004	**$61,280**	**$8,336**	**$23,316**	**$23,316**	**$0**	**1.00**	**$14,980**	**2.79**	**$61,280**	**1.00**	**$0**
WP-14	$30,260	$8,336	$23,316	$23,316	$0	1.00	$14,980	2.79	$30,260	1.00	$0
WP-15	$29,760								$29,760	1.00	$0
WP-16	$1,260								$1,260	1.00	$0
CA-005	**$13,700**								**$13,700**	**1.00**	**$0**
WP-17	$11,540								$11,540	1.00	$0
WP-18	$2,160								$2,160	1.00	$0
TOTAL	**$1,356,760**	**$542,789**	**$618,953**	**$622,272**	**$3,319**	**1.01**	**$79,483**	**1.00**	**$1,349,523**	**1.00**	**$7,237**

[A] Undefined (divided by zero).

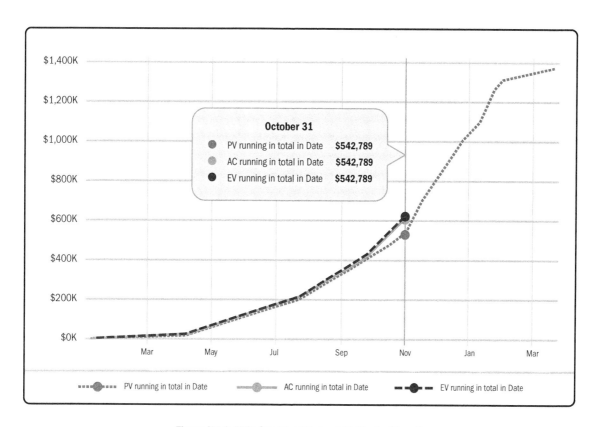

Figure X4-3. EVM Graphical Data at 44 Weeks (Year 1)

X4.4.4 WEEK 52 (YEAR 1)

The project is going well and the organization has other needs for the project controls team (see Table X4-5). In a meeting with senior company leaders, the team meets with the building managers who will be taking over the building. It is decided that the project controls team will move to WP-03 (Close Project Phase) 7 weeks early ($41,613.53 in scope value) in year 2's week 4, and the organization's building management team will execute CA-005 (Smart Building Handover Phase). Many of the building management team members used to work in the PMO and are very familiar with the handover phase activities. This management decision saves the organization over $40,000 by freeing up the project controls team to start on another project with little risk to the project.

Table X4-5. EVM Data at Week 52 (Year 1)

CA	BAC	PV	AC	EV	CV	CPI	SV	SPI	EAC$_{cpi}$	TCPI$_{bac}$	VAC
CA-001	$294,386	$237,996	$249,896	$237,996	($11,900)	0.95	$0	1.00	$309,106	1.27	($14,719)
WP-01	$19,840	$19,840	$20,832	$19,840	($992)	0.95	$0	1.00	$20,832	0.00	($992)
WP-02	$255,986	$218,156	$229,064	$218,156	($10,908)	0.95	$0	1.00	$268,786	1.41	($12,799)
WP-03	$18,560								$18,560	1.00	$0
CA-002	$67,700	$67,700	$54,057	$67,700	$13,643	1.25	$0	1.00	$54,057	0.00	$13,643
WP-04	$24,100	$24,100	$17,111	$24,100	$6,989	1.41	$0	1.00	$17,111	0.00	$6,989
WP-05	$24,100	$24,100	$17,111	$24,100	$6,989	1.41	$0	1.00	$17,111	0.00	$6,989
WP-06	$19,500	$19,500	$19,835	$19,500	($335)	0.98	$0	1.00	$19,835	0.00	($335)
CA-003	$878,080	$520,817	$603,173	$603,173	$0	1.00	$82,356	1.15	$878,080	1.00	$0
WP-07	$31,380	$31,380	$31,380	$31,380	$0	1.00	$0	1.00	$31,380	1.00	$0
WP-08	$380,760	$295,089	$337,925	$337,925	$0	1.00	$42,836	1.14	$380,760	1.00	$0
WP-09	$98,540	$54,197	$78,832	$78,832	$0	1.00	$24,635	1.45	$98,540	1.00	$0
WP-10	$119,080	$68,471	$83,356	$83,356	$0	1.00	$14,885	1.21	$119,080	1.00	$0
WP-11	$71,680	$71,680	$71,680	$71,680	$0	1.00	$0	1.00	$71,680	1.00	$0
WP-12	$173,600								$173,600	1.00	$0
WP-13	$3,040								$3,040	1.00	$0
CA-004	$60,020	$33,236	$48,116	$48,116	$0	1.00	$14,880	1.45	$60,020	1.00	$0
WP-14	$30,260	$30,260	$30,260	$30,260	$0	1.00	$0	1.00	$30,260	1.00	$0
WP-15	$29,760	$2,976	$17,856	$17,856	$0	1.00	$14,880	6.00	$29,760	1.00	$0
TOTAL	$1,300,186	$859,749	$955,242	$956,984	$1,743	1.00	$97,236	1.00	$1,299,818	0.99	$2,368

X4.4.5 WEEK 10 (YEAR 2)

The building management team completes CA-005 on time and within budget. The team could have accelerated the handover phase, but accelerating this activity was not needed.

X4.5 CLOSING A PROJECT USING EVM

As part of Close Project Phase (WP-03), the project controls team captures lessons learned (see Section 5). For the example project, the smart building, there are several lessons learned that were captured (see Table X4-6).

◆ If the program controls team is using new staff, more time might be needed. Therefore, an adjustment in the standards for estimating the team costs are going to be made.

- The goal of EVM is to achieve better cost and schedule performance in the accomplishment of work scope. But performance is not simply a function of execution; it depends also on the quality of planning and control.

- The organization moved CA-005 (Handover Phase) outside of the PMB so the control teams could complete closeout as the project came to an end. In this project, the building management team led the execution of CA-005 instead of the PMO and the project manager with very positive results. This option will be documented in the organization's OPA for consideration in future projects.

Table X4-6. Project Closing Data

CA	BAC	PV	AC	EV	CV	CPI	SV	SPI	EAC$_{cpi}$	TCPI$_{bac}$	VAC
CA-001	**$294,386**	**$294,386**	**$308,178**	**$294,386**	**($13,791)**	**0.96**	**$0**	**1.00**	**$308,178**	**0.00**	**($13,791)**
WP-01	$19,840	$19,840	$20,832	$19,840	($992)	0.95	$0	1.00	$20,832	0.00	($992)
WP-02	$255,986	$255,986	$268,786	$255,986	($12,799)	0.95	$0	1.00	$268,786	0.00	($12,799)
WP-03	$18,560	$18,560	$18,560	$18,560	$0	1.00	$0		$18,560	1.00	$0
CA-002	**$67,700**	**$67,700**	**$54,057**	**$67,700**	**$13,643**	**1.25**	**$0**	**1.00**	**$54,057**	**0.00**	**$13,643**
WP-04	$24,100	$24,100	$17,111	$24,100	$6,989	1.41	$0	1.00	$17,111	0.00	$6,989
WP-05	$24,100	$24,100	$17,111	$24,100	$6,989	1.41	$0	1.00	$17,111	0.00	$6,989
WP-06	$19,500	$19,500	$19,835	$19,500	($335)	0.98	$0	1.00	$19,835	0.00	($335)
CA-003	**$878,080**	**$878,080**	**$878,080**	**$878,080**	**$0**	**1.00**	**$0**	**1.00**	**$878,080**	**1.00**	**$0**
WP-07	$31,380	$31,380	$31,380	$31,380	$0	1.00	$0		$31,380	1.00	$0
WP-08	$380,760	$380,760	$380,760	$380,760	$0	1.00	$0	1.00	$380,760	1.00	$0
WP-09	$98,540	$98,540	$98,540	$98,540	$0	1.00	$0	1.00	$98,540	1.00	$0
WP-10	$119,080	$119,080	$119,080	$119,080	$0	1.00	$0	3.00	$119,080	1.00	$0
WP-11	$71,680	$71,680	$71,680	$71,680	$0	1.00	$0	1.00	$71,680	1.00	$0
WP-12	$173,600	$173,600	$173,600	$173,600	$0	1.00	$0	1.00	$173,600	1.00	$0
WP-13	$3,040	$3,040	$3,040	$3,040	$0	1.00	$0	1.00	$3,040	1.00	$0
CA-004	**$61,280**	**$61,280**	**$61,280**	**$61,280**	**$0**	**1.00**	**$0**	**1.00**	**$61,280**	**1.00**	**$0**
WP-14	$30,260	$30,260	$30,260	$30,260	$0	1.00	$0	1.00	$30,260	1.00	$0
WP-15	$29,760	$29,760	$29,760	$29,760	$0	1.00	$0	1.00	$29,760	1.00	$0
WP-16	$1,260	$1,260	$1,260	$1,260	$0	1.00	$0	1.00	$1,260	1.00	$0
CA-005	**$13,700**	**$13,700**	**$13,700**	**$13,700**	**$0**	**1.00**	**$0**	**1.00**	**$13,700**	**1.00**	**$0**
WP-17	$11,540	$11,540	$11,540	$11,540	$0	1.00	$0	1.00	$11,540	1.00	$0
WP-18	$2,160	$2,160	$2,160	$2,160	$0	1.00	$0	1.00	$2,160	1.00	$0
TOTAL	**$1,315,146**	**$1,315,146**	**$1,315,295**	**$1,315,146**	**($149)**	**1.00**	**$0**	**1.00**	**$1,315,295**	**0.00**	**($149)**

REFERENCES

[1]   Project Management Institute. 2017. *The PMI Lexicon of Project Management Terms.* Newtown Square, PA: Author.

[2]   Project Management Institute. 2017. *A Guide to the Project Management Body of Knowledge (PMBOK® Guide) –* Sixth Edition. Newtown Square, PA: Author.

[3]   Project Management Institute. 2017. *Agile Practice Guide.* Newtown Square, PA: Author.

[4]   Project Management Institute. 2017. *PMI's Pulse of the Profession®: Success Rates Rise—Transforming the High Cost of Low Performance.* Newtown Square, PA: Author.

[5]   Project Management Institute. 2017. *The Standard for Portfolio Management –* Fourth Edition. Newtown Square, PA: Author.

[6]   Project Management Institute. 2019. *The Standard for Risk Management in Portfolios, Programs, and Projects.* Newtown Square, PA: Author.

[7]   Project Management Institute. 2009. *Practice Standard for Project Risk Management.* Newtown Square, PA: Author.

[8]   Project Management Institute. 2019. *Practice Standard for Scheduling.* Newtown Square, PA: Author.

[9]   Project Management Institute. 2019. *Practice Standard for Project Estimating.* Newtown Square, PA: Author.

[10]   Project Management Institute. 2017. *Project Manager Competency Development Framework –* Third Edition. Newtown Square, PA: Author.

[11]   Project Management Institute. 2011. *Practice Standard for Earned Value Management –* Second Edition. Newtown Square, PA: Author.

[12]   Project Management Institute. 2017. *The Standard for Program Management –* Fourth Edition. Newtown Square, PA: Author.

[13]   Project Management Institute. 2019. *Benefits Realization Management: A Practice Guide.* Newtown Square, PA: Author.

[14]   Project Management Institute. 2016. *PMI Thought Leadership Series: Benefits Realization Management Framework.* Newtown Square, PA: Author.

BIBLIOGRAPHY

Anbari, Frank, Dennis Cioffi, and Ernest Forman. "Integrating Performance Measures for Effective Project and Program Portfolio Leadership." Paper presented at PMI Global Congress 2007—North America, Atlanta, GA, October 2007.

Association for Project Management. *Earned Value Management: APM Guidelines.* 2nd ed. Buckinghamshire: Association for Project Management, 2014.

Association for Project Management. *Earned Value Management Handbook.* Buckinghamshire: Association for Project Management, 2014.

Association for Project Management. *The Earned Value Management Compass.* Buckinghamshire: Association for Project Management, 2014.

Cable, John, Javier Ordonez, Gouthami Chintalapani, and Catherine Plaisant. "Project Portfolio Earned Value Management Using Treemaps." Paper presented at PMI Research Conference: Innovations, London, England, July 2004.

Driessnack, John. "Time to Update OMB Capital Programming Guidance." PMI White Paper, 2017. https://www.pmi.org/media/pmi/documents/public/pdf/white-papers/omb-capital-programming-guidance.pdf

Heinlein, J. W., Christopher Craig, John Perotti, Megan Pearson, Teressa Wooten, and Lucas Balderson. "Earned Value Management: A Driver of Organizational Strategy; The Power of EVM in Managing Project Portfolios for Strategic Results." Paper presented at PMI Global Congress 2012—North America, Vancouver, British Columbia, Canada, October 2012.

Humphreys, Gary. *Integrated Project Management and Earned Value.* Frederick, PA: Humphreys & Associates, 2017.

Kulathumani, Murali. *Breakthrough Project Portfolio Management: Achieving the Next Level of Capability and Optimization.* Plantation, FL: J. Ross Publishing, 2018.

Piney, Crispin. "Benefits Realization Compendium: Benefits Integration Techniques for Tracking, Execution and Realization." *PM World Journal* VII, no. 4 (May 2019). https://pmworldlibrary.net/wp-content/uploads/2019/05/pmwj81-May2019-Piney-Benefits-series-part-9-Benefits-Compendium.pdf

Piney, Crispin. *Earned Benefit Program Management: Aligning, Realizing, and Sustaining Strategy.* Boca Raton, FL: CRC Press, 2018.

Portfolio Management Framework (Section 2—Volume 3 of 3). "Report of the Advisory Panel on Streamlining and Codifying Acquisition Regulation," Section 809 Panel, DoD, January 2019.

Rodrigues, Alexandre. "Effective Measurement of Time Performance Using Earned Value Management: A Proposed Modified Version for SPI Tested Across Various Industries and Project Types." In *Advances in Project Management: Narrated Journeys in Unchartered Territory* edited by Darren Dalcher, 67–96. London: Gower Publishing, 2014.

Rodrigues, A. "Performance Management for Projects and Programs." Paper presented at the PMI Greece Chapter PM Symposium, Athens, 2019.

Serra, Carlos Eduardo Martins. *Benefits Realization Management: Strategic Value from Portfolios, Programs, and Projects.* Boca Raton, FL: CRC Press, 2017.

Tyler, M. Jeffery. *Practical Project EVM.* 2nd ed. Charleston, SC: Create Space, 2015.

Wolfert, Roel, and Roger Davies. "From Earned Value to Value Realization." *PM World Journal* VI, no. 9 (September 2015). https://pmworldlibrary.net/wp-content/uploads/2015/09/pmwj38-Sep2015-Wolfert-Davies-from-earned-value-to-value-realisation-Advances-Series.pdf

Wu, Te, and Panos Chatzipanos. *Implementing Portfolio Management.* Newtown Square, PA: Project Management Institute (PMI), 2018.

GLOSSARY

1. INCLUSIONS AND EXCLUSIONS

This glossary includes terms that are:

◆ Unique or nearly unique to project management (e.g., project scope statement, work package, work breakdown structure, critical path method).

◆ Not unique to project management, but used differently or with a narrower meaning in project management than in general everyday usage (e.g., early start date).

This glossary generally does not include:

◆ Application area-specific terms.

◆ Terms used in project management that do not differ in any material way from everyday use (e.g., calendar day, delay).

◆ Compound terms whose meaning is clear from the meanings of the component parts.

◆ Variants when the meaning of the variant is clear from the base term.

◆ Terms that are used only once and are not critical to understanding the point of the sentence. This can include a list of examples that would not have each term defined in the Glossary.

2. COMMON ACRONYMS

AC   actual cost

AT   actual time

BAC	budget at completion
CA	control account
CCB	change control board
CoP	community of practice
CPI	cost performance index
CR	contingency reserve
CV	cost variance
EAC	estimate at completion
EEF	enterprise environmental factor
ES	earned schedule
ETC	estimate to complete
EV	earned value
EVM	earned value management
EVMS	earned value management system
IEAC	independent estimate at completion
$IEAC_c$	independent estimate at completion expressed in cost
$IEAC_t$	independent estimate at completion expressed in time
IETC	independent estimate to complete
IPT	integrated project team
KPI	key performance indicator
LOE	level of effort
MR	management reserve
NTE	not to exceed
OBS	organizational breakdown structure

OPA	organizational process asset
OTB	over-target baseline
OTS	over-target schedule
PMB	performance measurement baseline
PMIS	project management information system
PMO	project management office
PV	planned value
RAM	responsibility assignment matrix
RCA	root cause analysis
SAC	schedule at completion
SME	subject matter expert
SPI	schedule performance index
SPI_t	schedule performance index expressed in time
SPI_w	schedule performance index expressed in work volume
SV	schedule variance
SV_t	schedule variance expressed in time
SV_w	schedule variance expressed in work volume
TCPI	to-complete cost performance index
TSPI	to-complete schedule performance index
UB	undistributed budget
VAC	variance at completion
WBS	work breakdown structure
WP	work package

3. DEFINITIONS

Actual Cost (AC). The realized cost incurred for the work performed on an activity during a specific time period. This can be reported for cumulative to date or for a specific reporting period.

Actual Time (AT). The number of time periods from the start of the project to the project status date.

Apportioned Effort (AE). The effort applied to project work that is not readily divisible into discrete efforts for that work, but which is related in direct proportion to measurable discrete work efforts. The value for the apportioned effort is determined based on the earned value of the corresponding discrete activity.

Budget at Completion (BAC). The sum of all the budgets established for the work to be performed on a project, work breakdown structure (WBS) component, control account (CA), or work package (WP). The project BAC is the sum of all work package BACs.

Change Control Board (CCB). A formally chartered group responsible for reviewing, evaluating, approving, delaying, or rejecting changes to the project, and for recording and communicating such decisions.

Control Account (CA). A management control point where scope, budget, actual cost, and schedule are integrated and compared to earned value for performance measurement. Each control account may be further decomposed into work packages and/or planning packages.

Control Account Manager. The manager within the project's organizational breakdown structure (OBS) that has been given the authority and responsibility to manage one or more control accounts.

Cost Performance Index (CPI). A measure of the cost efficiency of budgeted resources expressed as the ratio of earned value to actual cost: CPI = EV/AC.

Cost Variance (CV). The amount of budget deficit or surplus at a given point in time. It is the difference between earned value (EV) and actual cost (AC). CV = EV − AC. A positive value indicates a favorable condition and a negative value indicates an unfavorable condition.

Cumulative Velocity. The summation of the velocities for all completed iterations at a point in time. Cumulative velocity represents the earned value of the planned backlog achieved.

Discrete Effort. A work effort that can be planned and measured and that yields a specific output. Discrete effort is directly related to specific end products or services with distinct and measurable points, and outputs that result directly from the discrete effort.

Distributed Budget. The budget for project scope that has been identified to work breakdown structure (WBS) control accounts and also has an identified control account manager.

Earned Schedule (ES). An earned value technique that measures the time at which planned value equals earned value.

Earned Value (EV). The measure of the work performed, expressed in terms of the budget authorized for that work.

Earned Value Management (EVM). A methodology that combines scope, schedule, and resource measurements to assess project performance and progress.

Enterprise Environmental Factors (EEF). Conditions, not under the immediate control of the team, that influence, constrain, or direct the project, program, or portfolio.

Estimate at Completion (EAC). The expected total cost of completing all work expressed as the sum of the actual cost to date (AC) and the estimate to complete (ETC): $EAC = AC + ETC$.

Estimate at Completion (time) (EAC_t). The expected total time of completing project work. EAC_t is equal to the actual time (AT) plus the estimate to complete (time) (ETC_t) for the remaining work: $EAC_t = AT + ETC_t$.

Estimate to Complete (ETC). The estimated cost of completing the remaining work.

Independent Estimate at Completion (IEAC). A mathematical or statistical approach to project an EAC or a range of EACs using EVM data. These EAC calculations are independent of any future project or environmental conditions, and are not a replacement for a derived (bottom-up) project EAC.

Independent Estimate at Completion (time) ($IEAC_t$). A mathematical or statistical approach to calculate a project duration or range of durations using EVM data. Using earned schedule, the $IEAC_t$ is equal to the planned duration divided by SPI_t.

Independent Estimate to Complete (IETC). A mathematical or statistical approach to calculate a project completion date or range of completion dates using EVM data. The IETC is equal to the project start date plus the $IEAC_t$.

Level of Effort (LOE). A method of measurement used for support-type activities that does not produce definitive end products that can be delivered or measured objectively.

Organizational Breakdown Structure (OBS). A hierarchical representation of the project organization that illustrates the relationship between project activities and the organizational units that will perform those activities.

Organizational Process Assets (OPA). Plans, processes, policies, procedures, and knowledge bases that are specific to and used by the performing organization.

Performance Measurement Baseline (PMB). An approved, integrated scope-schedule-cost plan for the project work against which project execution is compared to measure and manage performance. The PMB includes contingency reserve (CR), but excludes management reserve (MR).

Planned Value (PV). The authorized budget assigned to scheduled work.

Planning Package. The work and budget that have been identified to a control account but are not yet defined into work packages.

Project Management Information System (PMIS). An information system consisting of the tools and techniques used to gather, integrate, and disseminate the outputs of project management processes.

Project Management Office (PMO). A management structure that standardizes the project-related governance processes and facilitates the sharing of resources, methodologies, tools, and techniques.

Responsibility Assignment Matrix (RAM). A structure that integrates the project organizational breakdown structure (OBS) with the work breakdown structure (WBS) to identify the control accounts.

Root Cause Analysis (RCA). An analytical technique used to determine the basic underlying reason(s) that causes a variance or a defect or a risk. A root cause may underlie more than one variance or defect or risk.

Schedule at Completion (SAC). The total schedule duration established to complete the entire work scope.

Schedule Performance Index (SPI). A measure of schedule efficiency expressed as the ratio of progress achieved to date as measured by the earned value (EV) to the planned progress expressed as planned value to date (PV): $SPI = EV/PV$.

Schedule Variance (SV). A measure of schedule performance on a project, expressed as the difference between earned value (EV) and planned value (PV): $SV = EV - PV$.

Summary-Level Budget. A time-phased budget for far-term work that is yet to mature to a level that can be reasonably planned and allocated to control accounts.

To-Complete Cost Performance Index (TCPI). A measure of the cost performance that must be achieved with the remaining resources in order to meet a specified management goal, such as the EAC or the BAC, expressed as: $TCPI = (BAC - EV) / (EAC - AC)$.

To-Complete Schedule Performance Index (TSPI). The calculated projection of schedule performance that must be achieved on remaining work to meet a specified goal, such as the EAC_t, expressed as $TSPI = (AC - EV) / (AC - PV)$.

Undistributed Budget (UB). The budget for project scope that has not yet been identified to work breakdown structure (WBS) elements and, below those, to control accounts. This budget has yet to be distributed to a responsible control account manager for detailed planning and time phasing.

Variance at Completion (VAC). A projection of the amount of budget deficit or surplus, expressed as the difference between the budget at completion (BAC) and the estimate at completion (EAC): $VAC = BAC - EAC$.

Variance Threshold. A predetermined range of normal outcomes that sets the acceptable performance boundaries within which the team practices management by exception. Generally established for cost variances (CV), schedule variances (SV), and variances at completion (VAC).

Work Breakdown Structure (WBS). A hierarchical decomposition of the total scope of work to be carried out by the project team to accomplish the project objectives and create the required deliverables.

Work Breakdown Structure (WBS) Dictionary. A document that provides detailed deliverable, activity, and schedule information about each component in the work breakdown structure.

Work Package (WP). The work defined at the lowest level of the work breakdown structure (WBS) for which cost and duration can be estimated and managed. Each work package has a unique scope of work, budget, scheduled start and completion dates, and may only belong to one control account.

INDEX

G

A Guide to the Project Management Body of Knowledge (*PMBOK® Guide*), 1, 4
    Closing, 105
    control account, 29
    EVM and, 5
    Initiating and, 17
    project charter considerations in, 18–19
    Project Cost Management, 37
    on project management plan, 30
    resource planning, 37–38
    risk management described by, 45–46
    risk planning, 39
    schedule planning, 32
    scope management and EVM, 31
    stakeholder and communications considerations, 95

H

Hybrid project, for EVM reporting, 97

I

IEAC. *See* Independent estimate at completion
$IEAC_c$. *See* Independent estimate at completion in cost
$IEAC_t$. *See* Independent estimate at completion in time
IETC. *See* Independent estimate to complete
Independent estimate at completion (IEAC), 90, 157
Independent estimate at completion in cost ($IEAC_c$), 87, 88
Independent estimate at completion in time ($IEAC_t$), 157
Independent estimate to complete (IETC), 90, 157
Initiating Process Group, 6, 17
Initiating processes
    EVMS applicability, 18–19, 21–26
    overview, 17–18
    project charter considerations, 18–19

    purpose of, 17
    stakeholder considerations, 19–20
Integrated change control
    change analysis, 100
    change requests, 99
    cost and schedule change analysis, 101
    EVM, 98–102
    rebaselining, 102
    scope change analysis, 100–101
Integrated project schedule, 60
Integrated project team (IPT), 45

K

Key performance indicators (KPI), 106
Knowledge Areas
    CA/WP breakout for planning, 29
    EVM uses with, 1
    Mapping with Process Groups, 6
Knowledge management, 108–109
KPI. *See* Key performance indicator

L

Level of detail, resource planning and, 38
Level of effort (LOE), 33, 34, 36, 157
LOE. *See* Level of effort

M

Management by exception, 71, 82, 95
Management control, 9, 29, 31
Management reserves (MR), 46–47
    PMB and, 55
Managing performance, EVM, 11–13, 71–95
    for agile, 91
    backlog impacts on PMB, 94
    calculating PV, EV, and AC within agile, 91–92